William Shakespeare's

The Merry Wives of Wi

In Plain and Simple English

 BOOKCAPS

BookCaps Study Guides
www.bookcaps.com

© 2012. All Rights Reserved.

Table of Contents

About This Series

The "Classic Retold" series started as a way of telling classics for the modern reader—being careful to preserve the themes and integrity of the original. Whether you want to understand Shakespeare a little more or are trying to get a better grasps of the Greek classics, there is a book waiting for you!

Characters

SIR JOHN FALSTAFF FENTON, a young gentleman

SHALLOW, a country justice

SLENDER, cousin to Shallow

FORD, Gentleman dwelling at Windsor

PAGE, Gentleman dwelling at Windsor

WILLIAM PAGE, a boy, son to Page

SIR HUGH EVANS, a Welsh parson

DOCTOR CAIUS, a French physician

HOST of the Garter Inn

BARDOLPH, PISTOL, NYM, Followers of Falstaff

ROBIN, page to Falstaff

SIMPLE, servant to Slender

RUGBY, servant to Doctor Caius

MISTRESS FORD MISTRESS PAGE MISTRESS ANNE PAGE, her daughter, in love with Fenton

MISTRESS QUICKLY, servant to Doctor Caius

SERVANTS to Page, Ford, &c.

Comparative Version

Act 1

SCENE I. Windsor. Before PAGE's house.

Enter SHALLOW, SLENDER, and SIR HUGH EVANS

SHALLOW
Sir Hugh, persuade me not; I will make a Star-chamber matter of it: if he were twenty Sir John Falstaffs, he shall not abuse Robert Shallow, esquire.

Sir Hugh, do not try and persuade me; I will make a high court case of it: if he were twenty Sir John Falstaffs, I would not allow him to abuse Robert Shallow, esquire.

SLENDER
In the county of Gloucester, justice of peace and 'Coram.'

In the county of Gloucester, justice of the peace and member of the bench.

SHALLOW
Ay, cousin Slender, and 'Custalourum.'

That's right, cousin Slender, and record keeper.

SLENDER
Ay, and 'Rato-lorum' too; and a gentleman born, master parson; who writes himself 'Armigero,' in any
bill, warrant, quittance, or obligation, 'Armigero.'

*Yes, and "decor reaper" as well; and a gentleman by birth,
a distinguished parson; who signs himself "Squire" on any
bill, warrant, release or contract, "Esq."*

SHALLOW
Ay, that I do; and have done any time these three hundred years.

Yes, I do; and I have done for donkey's years.

SLENDER
All his successors gone before him hath done't; and all his ancestors that come after him may: they may give the dozen white luces in their coat.

All his predecessors have done it; and all those who come after him may: they can have a dozen white pikes on their coat of arms.

SHALLOW
It is an old coat.

It is an old coat.

SIR HUGH EVANS
The dozen white louses do become an old coat well; it agrees well, passant; it is a familiar beast to man, and signifies love.

The dozen white lice do suit an old coat; they look very good, walking; men know them very well, and it shows you've been in love.

SHALLOW
The luce is the fresh fish; the salt fish is an old coat.

The pike is a freshwater fish; saltfish are old cod.

SLENDER
I may quarter, coz.

I may incorporate another coat of arms in mine, cousin.

SHALLOW
You may, by marrying.

You can, if you marry.

SIR HUGH EVANS
It is marring indeed, if he quarter it.

It would indeed be marring it, to incorporate another.

SHALLOW
Not a whit.

Not in the slightest.

SIR HUGH EVANS
Yes, py'r lady; if he has a quarter of your coat,
there is but three skirts for yourself, in my
simple conjectures: but that is all one. If Sir
John Falstaff have committed disparagements unto
you, I am of the church, and will be glad to do my
benevolence to make atonements and compremises
between you.

Yes, by our Lady; if someone has a quarter of your coat,
that only leaves three skirts for yourself, in my
simple arithmetic: but anyway. If Sir
John Falstaff has insulted you at all,
I am a churchman, and will be glad to be
a peacemaker to effect reconciliations and
compromises between you.

SHALLOW
The council shall hear it; it is a riot.

The court shall hear of it; he's started a riot.

SIR HUGH EVANS
It is not meet the council hear a riot; there is no
fear of Got in a riot: the council, look you, shall
desire to hear the fear of Got, and not to hear a
riot; take your vizaments in that.

It's not right for the court to hear a riot; there is no
fear of God in a riot: the council, understand, will
want to hear about the fear of God, and not a riot;
take that into consideration.

SHALLOW
Ha! o' my life, if I were young again, the sword
should end it.

Ha! I swear, if I were young again, we would settle
it
with swords.

SIR HUGH EVANS
It is petter that friends is the sword, and end it:
and there is also another device in my prain, which
peradventure prings goot discretions with it: there
is Anne Page, which is daughter to Master Thomas
Page, which is pretty virginity.

It is better to be settled with swords, and finish it:
I'm also thinking about something else,
which might result in some good things: there
is Anne Page, who is the daughter of Master
Thomas
Page, a pretty innocent.

SLENDER
Mistress Anne Page? She has brown hair, and
speaks
small like a woman.

Mistress Anne Page? She has brown hair, and
speaks
high like a woman.

SIR HUGH EVANS
It is that fery person for all the orld, as just as
you will desire; and seven hundred pounds of
moneys,
and gold and silver, is her grandsire upon his
death's-bed--Got deliver to a joyful resurrections!
--give, when she is able to overtake seventeen years
old: it were a goot motion if we leave our pribbles
and prabbles, and desire a marriage between Master
Abraham and Mistress Anne Page.

That's exactly the person I'm talking about, as good
as you could wish; and her grandfather (may he be
saved by God!) on his deathbed left her
seven hundred pounds in gold and silver,
which she will get when she is seventeen years
old: it would be a good idea to lay off our quibbles
and quarrels, and set up a marriage between
Master
Abraham and Mistress Anne Page.

SLENDER
Did her grandsire leave her seven hundred pound?

Did her grandfather leave her seven hundred pounds?

SIR HUGH EVANS
Ay, and her father is make her a petter penny.

Yes, and her father will make her richer still.

SLENDER
I know the young gentlewoman; she has good gifts.

I know the young gentlewoman; she has good qualities.

SIR HUGH EVANS
Seven hundred pounds and possibilities is goot gifts.

Seven hundred pounds with more to come are good qualities.

SHALLOW
Well, let us see honest Master Page. Is Falstaff there?

Well, let us go and see honest Master Page. Is Falstaff there?

SIR HUGH EVANS
Shall I tell you a lie? I do despise a liar as I do despise one that is false, or as I despise one that is not true. The knight, Sir John, is there; and, I beseech you, be ruled by your well-willers. I will peat the door for Master Page.

Should I lie to you? I hate liars the same as I hate people who are false, or as I hate people that are untruthful. The knight, Sir John, is there; and, I beg you, be guided by those who wish you well. I will knock for Master Page.

Knocks
What, hoa! Got pless your house here!

Hello there! God bless your house!

PAGE
[Within] Who's there?

Who's there?

Enter PAGE

SIR HUGH EVANS
Here is Got's plessing, and your friend, and Justice Shallow; and here young Master Slender, that peradventures shall tell you another tale, if matters grow to your likings.

God's blessing, and your friend, and Justice Shallow; and here is young Master Slender, who could maybe tell you a proverb, if things proceed to your liking.

PAGE
I am glad to see your worships well.
I thank you for my venison, Master Shallow.

*I'm glad to see your worships are well.
Thank you for my venison, Master Shallow.*

SHALLOW
Master Page, I am glad to see you: much good do it your good heart! I wished your venison better; it was ill killed. How doth good Mistress Page?--and I thank you always with my heart, la! with my heart.

Master Page, I'm glad to see you: I hope it does your good heart good! I wish your venison had been better; it was badly killed. How is the good Mistress Page?–And I always thank you with my heart, la! With my heart.

PAGE
Sir, I thank you.

Sir, I thank you.

SHALLOW
Sir, I thank you; by yea and no, I do.

Sir, I thank you; by golly I do.

PAGE
I am glad to see you, good Master Slender.

I'm glad to see you, good Master Slender.

SLENDER
How does your fallow greyhound, sir? I heard say he
was outrun on Cotsall.

*How's your pale brown greyhound, sir? I heard rumours he
was beaten at the Cotswold races.*

PAGE
It could not be judged, sir.

It was too close to call, sir.

SLENDER
You'll not confess, you'll not confess.

You won't admit it, you won't admit it.

SHALLOW
That he will not. 'Tis your fault, 'tis your fault;
'tis a good dog.

*He will not. It's your fault, it's your fault;
it's a good dog.*

PAGE
A cur, sir.

A mutt, sir.

SHALLOW
Sir, he's a good dog, and a fair dog: can there be
more said? he is good and fair. Is Sir John
Falstaff here?

*Sir, he's a good dog, and a good-looking dog: what
more can be said? He is good and good-looking. Is
Sir John Falstaff here?*

PAGE
Sir, he is within; and I would I could do a good
office between you.

*Sir, he is inside; I should like to do you both
a favour.*

SIR HUGH EVANS
It is spoke as a Christians ought to speak.

Spoken like a Christian.

SHALLOW
He hath wronged me, Master Page.

He has done me wrong, Master Page.

PAGE
Sir, he doth in some sort confess it.

Sir, he has kind of admitted it.

SHALLOW
If it be confessed, it is not redress'd: is not that
so, Master Page? He hath wronged me; indeed he
hath, at a word, he hath, believe me: Robert
Shallow, esquire, saith, he is wronged.

*He might have admitted it, but he has not made
amends: isn't that the case
Master Page? He has wronged me; he definitely
has, definitely, he has, believe me: Robert
Shallow, esquire, says he has been wronged.*

PAGE
Here comes Sir John.

Here comes Sir John.

Enter FALSTAFF, BARDOLPH, NYM, and PISTOL

FALSTAFF
Now, Master Shallow, you'll complain of me to the
king?

Now, Master Shallow, you're going to complain about me to the King?

SHALLOW
Knight, you have beaten my men, killed my deer,
and
broke open my lodge.

Sir, you have beaten my men, killed my deer, and broken into my lodge.

FALSTAFF
But not kissed your keeper's daughter?

But I didn't kiss your gamekeeper's daughter?

SHALLOW
Tut, a pin! this shall be answered.

That has nothing to do with it! You shall answer these charges.

FALSTAFF
I will answer it straight; I have done all this.
That is now answered.

I will answer them right now; I've done all these things. There, I have answered.

SHALLOW
The council shall know this.

The court shall hear of this.

FALSTAFF
'Twere better for you if it were known in counsel:
you'll be laughed at.

It would be best for you if it was heard in private: they'll laugh at you.

SIR HUGH EVANS
Pauca verba, Sir John; goot worts.

A few words, Sir John: good words.

FALSTAFF
Good worts! good cabbage. Slender, I broke your
head: what matter have you against me?

Good words! Good cabbage. Slender, I bashed you on the head: what complaints have you got against me?

SLENDER
Marry, sir, I have matter in my head against you;
and against your cony-catching rascals, Bardolph,
Nym, and Pistol.

Well, sir, I have the complaint about my head; and also about your cheating rascals, Bardolph, Nym, and Pistol.

BARDOLPH
You Banbury cheese!

You skinny rascal!

SLENDER
Ay, it is no matter.

Well, it doesn't matter.

PISTOL
How now, Mephostophilus!

What's this, you devil!

SLENDER

Ay, it is no matter.

NYM
Slice, I say! pauca, pauca: slice! that's my humour.

SLENDER
Where's Simple, my man? Can you tell, cousin?

SIR HUGH EVANS
Peace, I pray you. Now let us understand. There is three umpires in this matter, as I understand; that is, Master Page, fidelicet Master Page; and there is myself, fidelicet myself; and the three party is, lastly and finally, mine host of the Garter.

PAGE
We three, to hear it and end it between them.

SIR HUGH EVANS
Fery goot: I will make a prief of it in my note-book; and we will afterwards ork upon the cause with
as great discreetly as we can.

FALSTAFF
Pistol!

PISTOL
He hears with ears.

SIR HUGH EVANS
The tevil and his tam! what phrase is this, 'He hears with ear'? why, it is affectations.

FALSTAFF
Pistol, did you pick Master Slender's purse?

SLENDER
Ay, by these gloves, did he, or I would I might never come in mine own great chamber again else, of
seven groats in mill-sixpences, and two Edward shovel-boards, that cost me two shilling and two pence apiece of Yead Miller, by these gloves.

FALSTAFF
Is this true, Pistol?

SIR HUGH EVANS
No; it is false, if it is a pick-purse.

Well, it doesn't matter.

Chop him up, I say! Chop chop chop! That's what I fancy.

Where's my servant, Simple? Can you tell me, cousin?

Quiet, please. Now let us consider this. There are three umpires in this matter, as I understand it; those are,
Master Page, namely Master Page; and there is myself, namely myself; and third person is, lastly and finally, the landlord of the Garter.

Three of us, to hear the case and put an end to the quarrel.

Very good: I will make note of it in my notebook; afterwards we will consider the case with as much discretion as we can.

Pistol!

He listens with his ears.

The devil and worse! What does this mean, "he listens with his ears"? Why, it's an affectation.

Pistol, did you pinch Master Slender's purse?

Yes, by these gloves he did, if he didn't may I never enter my own bedroom again; there were seven groatsworth of silver sixpences, and two Edward
the Sixth shillings that cost me two shillings and tuppence
each from Ned Miller, by these gloves.

Is this true, Pistol?

No; if a pocket has been picked, it is false.

PISTOL
Ha, thou mountain-foreigner! Sir John and Master mine,
I combat challenge of this latten bilbo.
Word of denial in thy labras here!
Word of denial: froth and scum, thou liest!

Ha, you Welshman! Sir John and my master,
I reject the challenge of this tin sword.
Deny it with your lips!
Deny it: froth and scum, you are lying!

SLENDER
[pointing at Nym]
By these gloves, then, 'twas he.

Then I swear, it was him.

NYM
Be avised, sir, and pass good humours: I will say
'marry trap' with you, if you run the nuthook's
humour on me; that is the very note of it.

Be careful, sir, and mind how you go: if you
try and play the policeman with me, you might
fall into your own trap; that's the long and short of
it.

SLENDER
By this hat, then, he in the red face had it; for
though I cannot remember what I did when you
made me
drunk, yet I am not altogether an ass.

Well I swear by my hat, then, that the one with the
red face took it;
although I can't remember everything I did when
you made me
drunk, I'm not a complete ass.

FALSTAFF
What say you, Scarlet and John?

What have you got to say, Scarlet and John?

BARDOLPH
Why, sir, for my part I say the gentleman had drunk
himself out of his five sentences.

Why, sir, I would say that the gentleman was drunk
out of his five sentences.

SIR HUGH EVANS
It is his five senses: fie, what the ignorance is!

The phrase is "his five senses": my goodness, how
ignorant!

BARDOLPH
And being fap, sir, was, as they say, cashiered; and
so conclusions passed the careires.

And being drunk, Sir, was, as they say, fined; and
so things got out of hand.

SLENDER
Ay, you spake in Latin then too; but 'tis no
matter: I'll ne'er be drunk whilst I live again,
but in honest, civil, godly company, for this trick:
if I be drunk, I'll be drunk with those that have
the fear of God, and not with drunken knaves.

Yes, you spoke in Latin then as well; but it doesn't
matter: I'll never be drunk again as long as I live,
except in honest, civil, pious company, due to this
trick:
if I get drunk, I'll get drunk with those who have
the fear of God, and not with drunken knaves.

SIR HUGH EVANS
So Got 'urge me, that is a virtuous mind.

As God is my witness, that is a virtuous thought.

FALSTAFF
You hear all these matters denied, gentlemen; you
hear it.

You have heard all these allegations denied,
gentlemen; you have heard it.

Enter ANNE PAGE, with wine; MISTRESS FORD and MISTRESS PAGE, following

PAGE
Nay, daughter, carry the wine in; we'll drink within.

No, daughter, take the wine inside; we will drink it in there.

Exit ANNE PAGE

SLENDER
O heaven! this is Mistress Anne Page.

Good heavens! This is Mistress Anne Page.

PAGE
How now, Mistress Ford!

Hello there, Mistress Ford!

FALSTAFF
Mistress Ford, by my troth, you are very well met:
by your leave, good mistress.

Mistress Ford, upon my word, it's good to see you: with your permission, good mistress.

Kisses her

PAGE
Wife, bid these gentlemen welcome. Come, we have a
hot venison pasty to dinner: come, gentlemen, I hope
we shall drink down all unkindness.

*Wife, welcome these gentlemen. Come on, we have a hot venison pie for dinner: come, gentlemen, I hope
we can swallow our differences over a drink.*

Exeunt all except SHALLOW, SLENDER, and SIR HUGH EVANS

SLENDER
I had rather than forty shillings I had my Book of
Songs and Sonnets here.

*I would rather have my book of songs and sonnets here
than have forty shillings.*

Enter SIMPLE

How now, Simple! where have you been? I must wait
on myself, must I? You have not the Book of Riddles
about you, have you?

*Hello there, Simple! Where have you been? I have to
serve myself, do I? You haven't got the book of riddles
with you, have you?*

SIMPLE
Book of Riddles! why, did you not lend it to Alice
Shortcake upon All-hallowmas last, a fortnight
afore Michaelmas?

The book of riddles! Why, didn't you lend it to Alice Shortcake at last Halloween, a fortnight before Michaelmas?

SHALLOW
Come, coz; come, coz; we stay for you. A word with
you, coz; marry, this, coz: there is, as 'twere, a
tender, a kind of tender, made afar off by Sir Hugh

*Come on, cousin; come on, cousin; we are waiting for you. A word with you, cousin; in fact, this, cousin: there is, as it were,
a plan, a kind of plan, hatched by Sir Hugh*

here. Do you understand me?

SLENDER
Ay, sir, you shall find me reasonable; if it be so,
I shall do that that is reason.

SHALLOW
Nay, but understand me.

SLENDER
So I do, sir.

SIR HUGH EVANS
Give ear to his motions, Master Slender: I will
description the matter to you, if you be capacity of
it.

SLENDER
Nay, I will do as my cousin Shallow says: I pray
you, pardon me; he's a justice of peace in his
country, simple though I stand here.

SIR HUGH EVANS
But that is not the question: the question is
concerning your marriage.

SHALLOW
Ay, there's the point, sir.

SIR HUGH EVANS
Marry, is it; the very point of it; to Mistress Anne
Page.

SLENDER
Why, if it be so, I will marry her upon any
reasonable demands.

SIR HUGH EVANS
But can you affection the 'oman? Let us command
to
know that of your mouth or of your lips; for divers
philosophers hold that the lips is parcel of the
mouth. Therefore, precisely, can you carry your
good will to the maid?

SHALLOW
Cousin Abraham Slender, can you love her?

SLENDER
I hope, sir, I will do as it shall become one that

---

here. Do you understand me?

*Yes, sir, you will find me understanding; if I am
I shall do what is understandable.*

No, you must understand me.

I do, sir.

*Listen to what he says, Master Slender: I will
explain the matter to you, if you can understand it.*

*No, I will do as my cousin Shallow says: I beg you
excuse me; he's a justice of the peace in his
neck of the woods, as true as I'm standing here.*

*But that's not what we're talking about: the subject
is your marriage.*

Yes, that's the thing, sir.

*Indeed, it is; absolutely the subject; to Mistress
Anne Page.*

*Well, if that's the case, I will marry her under any
reasonable conditions.*

*But can you capture the woman's affections? We
want to
hear the sort of thing that will come from your
mouth or your lips; for many scientists say that the
lips are part of the mouth. So, tell us exactly, can
you convince the girl that you love her?*

Cousin Abraham Slender, can you love her?

I hope, sir, I will do it in the manner of someone

would do reason.

SIR HUGH EVANS
Nay, Got's lords and his ladies! you must speak
possitable, if you can carry her your desires
towards her.

SHALLOW
That you must. Will you, upon good dowry, marry
her?

SLENDER
I will do a greater thing than that, upon your
request, cousin, in any reason.

SHALLOW
Nay, conceive me, conceive me, sweet coz: what I
do
is to pleasure you, coz. Can you love the maid?

SLENDER
I will marry her, sir, at your request: but if there
be no great love in the beginning, yet heaven may
decrease it upon better acquaintance, when we are
married and have more occasion to know one
another;
I hope, upon familiarity will grow more contempt:
but if you say, 'Marry her,' I will marry her; that
I am freely dissolved, and dissolutely.

SIR HUGH EVANS
It is a fery discretion answer; save the fall is in
the ort 'dissolutely:' the ort is, according to our
meaning, 'resolutely:' his meaning is good.

SHALLOW
Ay, I think my cousin meant well.

SLENDER
Ay, or else I would I might be hanged, la!

SHALLOW
Here comes fair Mistress Anne.

Re-enter ANNE PAGE

Would I were young for your sake, Mistress Anne!

ANNE PAGE
The dinner is on the table; my father desires your

---

doing the right thing.

*No, God's lords and his ladies! You must speak
positively, if you are going to convince her
of your desire.*

*That's right. Will you, if you get a good dowry,
marry her?*

*I will do bigger things that, if you ask me,
cousin, for any reason.*

*No, understand me, understand me, sweet cousin:
what I'm doing
is for your pleasure, cousin. Can you love the girl?*

*I will marry her, sir, if you ask me: but if there
is no great love at the beginning, then heaven may
make it even less as we get better acquainted, when
we are
married and have more chances to see each other;
I hope that familiarity will breed contempt:
but if you say, "marry her," I will marry her;
I've made my mind up to that, dissolutely.*

*That is a very good answer; except there's a mistake
in
the word "dissolutely": the word you want is
"resolutely": but his meaning is good.*

Yes, I think my cousin meant well.

Yes I did, or otherwise may I be hanged, ha!

Here comes lovely Mistress Anne.

You make me wish I was young, Mistress Anne!

Dinner is on the table; my father asks for

worships' company.

your worships to join him.

SHALLOW
I will wait on him, fair Mistress Anne.

I will be there, lovely Mistress Anne.

SIR HUGH EVANS
Od's plessed will! I will not be absence at the grace.

God be praised! I won't miss the grace.

Exeunt SHALLOW and SIR HUGH EVANS

ANNE PAGE
Will't please your worship to come in, sir?

Would you like to come in now, sir?

SLENDER
No, I thank you, forsooth, heartily; I am very well.

No, indeed, many thanks; I'm fine.

ANNE PAGE
The dinner attends you, sir.

Dinner is waiting for you, sir.

SLENDER
I am not a-hungry, I thank you, forsooth. Go,
sirrah, for all you are my man, go wait upon my
cousin Shallow.

I'm not hungry, thank you, indeed. Go,
sir, although you are my servant, go and wait on
my cousin Shallow.

Exit SIMPLE

A justice of peace sometimes may be beholding to
his
friend for a man. I keep but three men and a boy
yet, till my mother be dead: but what though? Yet I
live like a poor gentleman born.

A justice of the peace might sometimes lend his
friend a servant. I just employ three men and a boy
now, until my mother is dead: what about it? But I
live as though I was born poor.

ANNE PAGE
I may not go in without your worship: they will not
sit till you come.

I can't go back without your worship: they will not
begin until you come.

SLENDER
I' faith, I'll eat nothing; I thank you as much as
though I did.

I swear, I'll eat nothing: but I thank you
just the same.

ANNE PAGE
I pray you, sir, walk in.

Please sir, come in.

SLENDER
I had rather walk here, I thank you. I bruised
my shin th' other day with playing at sword and
dagger with a master of fence; three veneys for a
dish of stewed prunes; and, by my troth, I cannot
abide the smell of hot meat since. Why do your
dogs bark so? be there bears i' the town?

I'd rather stay out here, thank you. I bruised
my shin the other day in a sword and dagger fight
with a fencing master; we had three bouts for a bet
for a dish of stewed prunes, and I swear I haven't
been able to stand the smell of cooked meats since.
Why are your dogs barking like that? Are there

ANNE PAGE
I think there are, sir; I heard them talked of.

SLENDER
I love the sport well but I shall as soon quarrel at
it as any man in England. You are afraid, if you see
the bear loose, are you not?

ANNE PAGE
Ay, indeed, sir.

SLENDER
That's meat and drink to me, now. I have seen
Sackerson loose twenty times, and have taken him
by
the chain; but, I warrant you, the women have so
cried and shrieked at it, that it passed: but women,
indeed, cannot abide 'em; they are very ill-favored
rough things.

Re-enter PAGE

PAGE
Come, gentle Master Slender, come; we stay for
you.

SLENDER
I'll eat nothing, I thank you, sir.

PAGE
By cock and pie, you shall not choose, sir! come,
come.

SLENDER
Nay, pray you, lead the way.

PAGE
Come on, sir.

SLENDER
Mistress Anne, yourself shall go first.

ANNE PAGE
Not I, sir; pray you, keep on.

SLENDER
I'll rather be unmannerly than troublesome.
You do yourself wrong, indeed, la!

bears in town?

*I think there are, sir; I heard people talking about
them.*

*I love bear bating but I will have a quarrel at
it as quickly as any man in England. You are afraid,
if you see
the bear on the loose, aren't you?*

Yes, indeed, sir.

*Now that means nothing to me. I have seen
the bear Sackerson loose twenty times, and have
grabbed
his chain; but, I promise you, the women screamed
and cried at it so much, it was amazing: but women
certainly can't stand them; they are very ugly
rough things.*

*Come in, gentle Master Slender, come in; we are
waiting for you.*

Thank you, sir, I don't want anything to eat.

*By cock and pie, you shall not choose, sir! Come
on, come on.*

No, please, you lead the way.

Come on, sir.

Mistress Anne, after you.

Not me, sir; please, you go ahead.

*I'd rather be rude then cause trouble.
You are putting yourself down, really, ha ha!*

Exeunt

SCENE II. The same.

Enter SIR HUGH EVANS and SIMPLE

SIR HUGH EVANS
Go your ways, and ask of Doctor Caius' house
which
is the way: and there dwells one Mistress Quickly,
which is in the manner of his nurse, or his dry
nurse, or his cook, or his laundry, his washer, and
his wringer.

Go about your business, and ask the way to Doctor Caius'
house: someone called Mistress Quickly lives there,
she is his nurse, or his dry nurse,
or his cook, or his laundry woman, his dishwasher,
and his clothes dryer.

SIMPLE
Well, sir.

Good, sir.

SIR HUGH EVANS
Nay, it is petter yet. Give her this letter; for it
is a 'oman that altogether's acquaintance with
Mistress Anne Page: and the letter is, to desire
and require her to solicit your master's desires to
Mistress Anne Page. I pray you, be gone: I will
make an end of my dinner; there's pippins and
cheese to come.

No, we'll make it better. Give her this letter; this
woman is very well acquainted with
Mistress Anne Page: and the letter is asking
and ordering her to represent your master's feelings
to Mistress Anne Page. Please, go: I will
stay and finish my dinner: there's apples and cheese
to finish.

Exeunt

SCENE III. A room in the Garter Inn.

Enter FALSTAFF, Host, BARDOLPH, NYM, PISTOL, and ROBIN

FALSTAFF
Mine host of the Garter!

Host
What says my bully-rook? speak scholarly and
wisely.

FALSTAFF
Truly, mine host, I must turn away some of my
followers.

Host
Discard, bully Hercules; cashier: let them wag; trot,
trot.

FALSTAFF
I sit at ten pounds a week.

Host
Thou'rt an emperor, Caesar, Keisar, and Pheezar. I
will entertain Bardolph; he shall draw, he shall
tap: said I well, bully Hector?

FALSTAFF
Do so, good mine host.

Host
I have spoke; let him follow.

To BARDOLPH
Let me see thee froth and lime: I am at a word;
follow.

Exit

FALSTAFF
Bardolph, follow him. A tapster is a good trade:
an old cloak makes a new jerkin; a withered
serving-man a fresh tapster. Go; adieu.

BARDOLPH
It is a life that I have desired: I will thrive.

PISTOL
O base Hungarian wight! wilt thou the spigot wield?

Landlord of the Garter!

What's up you old devil? Speak intellectually and cleverly.

To tell the truth, landlord, I will have to lay off some of my followers.

Throw them off, good Hercules; sack them; let them hang; trot, trot.

I lodge at ten pounds a week.

You are an emperor, Caesar, Kaiser and Sultan. I will take on Bardolph; he can serve the beer: is this a good idea, good Hector?

Go ahead, my good host.

I have offered; let him take it up.

Let's see you in action: I don't waste words; follow me.

Bardolph, follow him. Tending bar is a good trade: you can make a new waistcoat out of an old cloak; a decrepit servant can make a new barman. Go; good luck.

That's a life I've always wanted: I will do well.

You low-down loser! So you'll work the beer pump?

Exit BARDOLPH

NYM
He was gotten in drink: is not the humour
conceited?

*He was conceived by drunkards: don't things come
round amusingly?*

FALSTAFF
I am glad I am so acquit of this tinderbox: his
thefts were too open; his filching was like an
unskilful singer; he kept not time.

*I'm glad to be rid of this troublemaker: his
thefts were too obvious; his stealing was like
an unskilful singer; he was off the beat.*

NYM
The good humour is to steal at a minute's rest.

The good thief steals at a pause in the music.

PISTOL
'Convey,' the wise it call. 'Steal!' foh! a fico
for the phrase!

*The wise call it "redistribution". "Stealing!" Pah!
Damn the phrase.*

FALSTAFF
Well, sirs, I am almost out at heels.

Well, gentlemen, I am very down at heel.

PISTOL
Why, then, let kibes ensue.

Well then, you'll get chilblains.

FALSTAFF
There is no remedy; I must cony-catch; I must shift.

*There is no cure for it; I must catch rabbits; I must
make do.*

PISTOL
Young ravens must have food.

The birds must be fed.

FALSTAFF
Which of you know Ford of this town?

Which of you know Ford, who lives in this town?

PISTOL
I ken the wight: he is of substance good.

I know the fellow: he's got plenty.

FALSTAFF
My honest lads, I will tell you what I am about.

My good lads, I'll tell you what I'm about.

PISTOL
Two yards, and more.

Two yards and more.

FALSTAFF
No quips now, Pistol! Indeed, I am in the waist two
yards about; but I am now about no waste; I am
about
thrift. Briefly, I do mean to make love to Ford's
wife: I spy entertainment in her; she discourses,
she carves, she gives the leer of invitation: I
can construe the action of her familiar style; and

*No jokes now, Pistol! It's true that I am two yards
around the waist; but I'm not talking about waste
now, I am talking about profit. In brief, I intend to
sweet talk Ford's wife. I can see a saucy spirit in
her; she chats,
she simpers, she gives inviting looks: I
know what all her actions mean; and*

the hardest voice of her behavior, to be Englished
rightly, is, 'I am Sir John Falstaff's.'

*all her behaviour cries out, in plain English,
"I am Sir John Falstaff's."*

PISTOL
He hath studied her will, and translated her will,
out of honesty into English.

*He's looked at her assets, and interpreted her
wants, into English out of honesty.*

NYM
The anchor is deep: will that humour pass?

She is well settled: can you get past that?

FALSTAFF
Now, the report goes she has all the rule of her
husband's purse: he hath a legion of angels.

*Now, it's said that she has control over her
husband's finances: and he has a sackful.*

PISTOL
As many devils entertain; and 'To her, boy,' say I.

You want to get in that sack then; go for it, I say.

NYM
The humour rises; it is good: humour me the angels.

*Yes I like this plan, it's a good one: let's hope it
turns out well.*

FALSTAFF
I have writ me here a letter to her: and here
another to Page's wife, who even now gave me good
eyes too, examined my parts with most judicious
oeillades; sometimes the beam of her view gilded
my
foot, sometimes my portly belly.

*I've got a letter here which I've written her: and
here is another one to Page's wife, who was
recently flirting with me too, looking me over with
very saucy eyes; sometimes she casts the sunbeam
of her look over
my feet, sometimes over my round belly.*

PISTOL
Then did the sun on dunghill shine.

Then the sun was shining on a dung heap.

NYM
I thank thee for that humour.

Nice joke.

FALSTAFF
O, she did so course o'er my exteriors with such a
greedy intention, that the appetite of her eye did
seem to scorch me up like a burning-glass! Here's
another letter to her: she bears the purse too; she
is a region in Guiana, all gold and bounty. I will
be cheater to them both, and they shall be
exchequers to me; they shall be my East and West
Indies, and I will trade to them both. Go bear thou
this letter to Mistress Page; and thou this to
Mistress Ford: we will thrive, lads, we will thrive.

*Oh, she ran her gaze over my appearance with such
a greedy look, that I thought I would burn up, as if
her eye was a magnifying glass! Here's
a letter for her: she controls the finances too; she
is a promised land, full of gold and profits. I will
be a taxman to both of them, and they shall be my
taxpayers; they'll be the East and West
Indies, and I will make trade voyages to both of
them. Go and take this letter to Mistress Page; and
you take this to Mistress Ford: we will do well my
lads, we will do well.*

PISTOL
Shall I Sir Pandarus of Troy become,
And by my side wear steel? then, Lucifer take all!

*Do I, a soldier, have to act as a pimp?
Devil take it all!*

NYM
I will run no base humour: here, take the
humour-letter: I will keep the havior of reputation.

I don't want to lower myself to this: take
your low letter: I will keep my reputation.

FALSTAFF
[To ROBIN] Hold, sirrah, bear you these letters
tightly;
Sail like my pinnace to these golden shores.
Rogues, hence, avaunt! vanish like hailstones, go;
Trudge, plod away o' the hoof; seek shelter, pack!
Falstaff will learn the humour of the age,
French thrift, you rogues; myself and skirted page.

Just a minute, lad, deliver those letters faithfully;
you're my ship taking me to golden shores.
You rascals, get out of here, off you go! Melt away
like hailstones, go;
go on, hoof it; get packing!
Falstaff will follow the fashion of the time,
French economy, you scoundrels, just me and a
page will be my whole household.

Exeunt FALSTAFF and ROBIN

PISTOL
Let vultures gripe thy guts! for gourd and fullam
holds,
And high and low beguiles the rich and poor:
Tester I'll have in pouch when thou shalt lack,
Base Phrygian Turk!

May vultures gnaw your guts! The loaded dice are
rolling,
and the rich and poor are both tricked:
I'll have sixpence in my purse when you have
nothing, you Turkish pimp!

NYM
I have operations which be humours of revenge.

I have a plan to get him back for this.

PISTOL
Wilt thou revenge?

You want revenge?

NYM
By welkin and her star!

By the sky and stars above!

PISTOL
With wit or steel?

With cunning or force?

NYM
With both the humours, I:
I will discuss the humour of this love to Page.

With my cunning and someone else's force:
I will reveal this love to Page.

PISTOL
And I to Ford shall eke unfold
How Falstaff, varlet vile,
His dove will prove, his gold will hold,
And his soft couch defile.

And I will tell Ford
how the horrible scoundrel Falstaff
wants to get his hands on his wife and his gold,
and pollute his bed.

NYM
My humour shall not cool: I will incense Page to
deal with poison; I will possess him with
yellowness, for the revolt of mine is dangerous:
that is my true humour.

I won't let this go: I will spur Page on to
be properly vicious; I will fill him with
jealousy, for mine is dangerous:
my mind is made up.

PISTOL
Thou art the Mars of malecontents: I second thee;
troop on.

You are the god of the wars of rebels: I'll back you up; march on.

Exeunt

SCENE IV. A room in DOCTOR CAIUS' house.

Enter MISTRESS QUICKLY, SIMPLE, and RUGBY

MISTRESS QUICKLY
What, John Rugby! I pray thee, go to the casement,
and see if you can see my master, Master Doctor
Caius, coming. If he do, i' faith, and find any
body in the house, here will be an old abusing of
God's patience and the king's English.

Where are you, John Rugby! Please, go to the
window, and see if you can see my master, Doctor
Caius, coming. If he does, and finds anybody
in the house, there will be a good deal of
wicked deeds and swearing.

RUGBY
I'll go watch.

I'll keep watch.

MISTRESS QUICKLY
Go; and we'll have a posset for't soon at night, in
faith, at the latter end of a sea-coal fire.
An honest, willing, kind fellow, as ever servant
shall come in house withal, and, I warrant you, no
tell-tale nor no breed-bate: his worst fault is,
that he is given to prayer; he is something peevish
that way: but nobody but has his fault; but let
that pass. Peter Simple, you say your name is?

Go; and later we'll have some toddy, I promise,
in front of a roaring fire.
As honest, hard-working and kind a servant
that ever came in to a house, and, I'll swear,
no tell-tale or mischief maker: his worst fault is
that he likes to pray; he's rather silly in
that way: but everybody has faults; we'll let
it go. Peter Simple, you say your name is?

Exit RUGBY

SIMPLE
Ay, for fault of a better.

Yes, lacking a better one.

MISTRESS QUICKLY
And Master Slender's your master?

And Master Slender's your master?

SIMPLE
Ay, forsooth.

Yes, indeed.

MISTRESS QUICKLY
Does he not wear a great round beard, like a
glover's paring-knife?

Doesn't he have a great round beard, shaped like a
leather cutter's knife?

SIMPLE
No, forsooth: he hath but a little wee face, with a
little yellow beard, a Cain-coloured beard.

Certainly not: he's just got a small face, with a
little yellow beard, reddish yellow.

MISTRESS QUICKLY
A softly-sprighted man, is he not?

Quite a gentle spirited man, isn't he?

SIMPLE
Ay, forsooth: but he is as tall a man of his hands
as any is between this and his head; he hath fought

Yes, indeed: but he is as good with his hands
as any man in the neighbourhood; he has fought

with a warrener.

MISTRESS QUICKLY
How say you? O, I should remember him: does he not
hold up his head, as it were, and strut in his gait?

You don't say? Oh, I should remember him: doesn't he
sort of look down his nose, and strut as he walks?

SIMPLE
Yes, indeed, does he.

He certainly does.

MISTRESS QUICKLY
Well, heaven send Anne Page no worse fortune! Tell
Master Parson Evans I will do what I can for your
master: Anne is a good girl, and I wish--

Well, I hope heaven doesn't send Anne Page
anything worse!
Tell Master Parson Evans that I will do what I can for your
master: Anne is a good girl, and I wish–

Re-enter RUGBY

RUGBY
Out, alas! here comes my master.

Alas, we're found out! Here comes my master.

MISTRESS QUICKLY
We shall all be shent. Run in here, good young man;
go into this closet: he will not stay long.

We are all in the soup. Jump in here, good lad;
go into this cupboard, he won't stay long.

Shuts SIMPLE in the closet
What, John Rugby! John! what, John, I say!
Go, John, go inquire for my master; I doubt
he be not well, that he comes not home.

Hey, John Rugby! John! Hey, John, I say!
John, go and ask where your master is; I worry
that he's not well, as he has not come home.

Singing
And down, down, adown-a, & c.

And down, down, adown-a, etc.

Enter DOCTOR CAIUS

DOCTOR CAIUS
Vat is you sing? I do not like des toys. Pray you,
go and vetch me in my closet un boitier vert, a box,
a green-a box: do intend vat I speak? a green-a box.

What are you singing? I don't like these frivolities.
Please, go and get a box green from my cupboard, a
box, green–a box: do understand what I'm saying?
A green box.

MISTRESS QUICKLY
Ay, forsooth; I'll fetch it you.

Yes, certainly; I'll get it for you.

Aside
I am glad he went not in himself: if he had found
the young man, he would have been horn-mad.

I'm glad he didn't go in himself: if he had found
the young man, he would have been mad with
jealousy.

DOCTOR CAIUS
Fe, fe, fe, fe! ma foi, il fait fort chaud. Je
m'en vais a la court--la grande affaire.

Fe, fe, fe, fe! My goodness, it's hot.
I've got to go and see important business at court.

MISTRESS QUICKLY
Is it this, sir?

Is this the one, sir?

DOCTOR CAIUS
Oui; mette le au mon pocket: depeche, quickly.
Vere
is dat knave Rugby?

*Yes; put it in my pocket: hurry up, be quick. Where
is that knave Rugby?*

MISTRESS QUICKLY
What, John Rugby! John!

Hey, John Rugby! John!

RUGBY
Here, sir!

Here, sir!

DOCTOR CAIUS
You are John Rugby, and you are Jack Rugby.
Come,
take-a your rapier, and come after my heel to the
court.

*You are John Rugby, and you are Idiot Rugby.
Come on;
bring your sword, and follow me to the court.*

RUGBY
'Tis ready, sir, here in the porch.

I have it ready, sir, here in the porch.

DOCTOR CAIUS
By my trot, I tarry too long. Od's me!
Qu'ai-j'oublie! dere is some simples in my closet,
dat I vill not for the varld I shall leave behind.

*By God, I'm late. Good heavens!
What have I forgotten! There are some medicines
in my cupboard
that I would not leave behind for the world.*

MISTRESS QUICKLY
Ay me, he'll find the young man here, and be mad!

*Oh no, he'll find the young man in there, and go
mad!*

DOCTOR CAIUS
O diable, diable! vat is in my closet? Villain! larron!

*Oh the devil, devil! What's this in my cupboard?
Villain! Thief!*

Pulling SIMPLE out

Rugby, my rapier!

Rugby, bring my sword!

MISTRESS QUICKLY
Good master, be content.

Good master, calm down.

DOCTOR CAIUS
Wherefore shall I be content-a?

And why should I be calm?

MISTRESS QUICKLY
The young man is an honest man.

This young man is an honest man.

DOCTOR CAIUS
What shall de honest man do in my closet? dere is
no honest man dat shall come in my closet.

*What's an honest man doing in my cupboard? There
is no honest man who would be in my cupboard.*

MISTRESS QUICKLY
I beseech you, be not so phlegmatic. Hear the truth
of it: he came of an errand to me from Parson Hugh.

*I beg you, don't be so hotheaded. Listen to the truth
of the matter: he came to me on an errand from
Parson Hugh.*

DOCTOR CAIUS
Vell.

Well.

SIMPLE
Ay, forsooth; to desire her to--

Yes, indeed; to ask her to—

MISTRESS QUICKLY
Peace, I pray you.

Be quiet, please.

DOCTOR CAIUS
Peace-a your tongue. Speak-a your tale.

You keep your mouth shut. Tell your story.

SIMPLE
To desire this honest gentlewoman, your maid, to
speak a good word to Mistress Anne Page for my
master in the way of marriage.

*To ask this honest gentlewoman, your maid, to
put in a good word to Mistress Anne Page for my
master in the matter of marriage.*

MISTRESS QUICKLY
This is all, indeed, la! but I'll ne'er put my
finger in the fire, and need not.

*Yes, that's all it was! But I'll never
get involved with that sort of thing, and don't have
to.*

DOCTOR CAIUS
Sir Hugh send-a you? Rugby, baille me some paper.
Tarry you a little-a while.

*Sir Hugh sent you? Rugby, bring me some paper.
You wait a little while.*

Writes

MISTRESS QUICKLY
[Aside to SIMPLE] I am glad he is so quiet: if he
had been thoroughly moved, you should have heard
him
so loud and so melancholy. But notwithstanding,
man, I'll do you your master what good I can: and
the very yea and the no is, the French doctor, my
master,--I may call him my master, look you, for I
keep his house; and I wash, wring, brew, bake,
scour, dress meat and drink, make the beds and do
all myself,--

*I am glad he is so calm: if he
had really been stirred up, you would have heard
him
very loud and wailing. But nevertheless,
man, I'll do the best I can for your master: and
the long and the short of it is, the French doctor, my
master—I may call him my master, you see, for I
am his housekeeper; and I wash, dry, brew, bake,
scrub, prepare meat and drink, make the beds and
do everything myself—*

SIMPLE
[Aside to MISTRESS QUICKLY] 'Tis a great
charge to
come under one body's hand.

That's a lot of work for one person.

MISTRESS QUICKLY
[Aside to SIMPLE] Are you avised o' that? you

You think so? You will find it

shall find it a great charge: and to be up early
and down late; but notwithstanding,--to tell you in
your ear; I would have no words of it,--my master
himself is in love with Mistress Anne Page: but
notwithstanding that, I know Anne's mind,--that's
neither here nor there.

*plenty of work: you have to get up early
and go to bed late; but nevertheless–I'll whisper
to you, I don't want it to get around–my master
is in love with Mistress Anne Page himself: but
nevertheless, I know Anne's mind–that's
neither here nor there.*

DOCTOR CAIUS
You jack'nape, give-a this letter to Sir Hugh; by
gar, it is a shallenge: I will cut his troat in dee
park; and I will teach a scurvy jack-a-nape priest
to meddle or make. You may be gone; it is not good
you tarry here. By gar, I will cut all his two
stones; by gar, he shall not have a stone to throw
at his dog:

*You monkey, give this letter to Sir Hugh; by
God, it is a challenge: I will cut his throat in the
park; and I will teach a rotten ape of a priest
to stick his nose in. You may go; I don't want you
hanging around. By God, I will chop off his
parts; by God, he won't have enough left
to feed his dog.*

Exit SIMPLE

MISTRESS QUICKLY
Alas, he speaks but for his friend.

He is only speaking for his friend.

DOCTOR CAIUS
It is no matter-a ver dat: do not you tell-a me
dat I shall have Anne Page for myself? By gar, I
vill kill de Jack priest; and I have appointed mine
host of de Jarteer to measure our weapon. By gar, I
will myself have Anne Page.

*That's not the problem: didn't you tell me
that I would have Anne Page for myself? By God,
I will kill that ape of a priest; and I have appointed
the landlord of the Garter to be my second. By God,
I will have Anne Page myself.*

MISTRESS QUICKLY
Sir, the maid loves you, and all shall be well. We
must give folks leave to prate: what, the good-jer!

*Sir, the girl loves you, and everything will be all
right.
We must allow people to talk, what the hell!*

DOCTOR CAIUS
Rugby, come to the court with me. By gar, if I have
not Anne Page, I shall turn your head out of my
door. Follow my heels, Rugby.

*Rugby, come to the court with me. By God, if I do
not
get Anne Page, I will throw you out.
Follow close behind, Rugby.*

Exeunt DOCTOR CAIUS and RUGBY

MISTRESS QUICKLY
You shall have An [exeunt Caius and Rugby] fool's-
head of your own. No, I
know Anne's mind for that: never a woman in
Windsor
knows more of Anne's mind than I do; nor can do
more
than I do with her, I thank heaven.

*You shall have An [Caius and Rugby leave] fool's–
head of your own. No,
I know what Anne thinks about it: no woman in
Windsor
knows more about Anne's feelings than I do; and
nobody
has a greater influence on her, thank heavens.*

FENTON
[Within] Who's within there? ho!

Hello! Is there anybody home?

MISTRESS QUICKLY
Who's there, I trow! Come near the house, I pray you.

Enter FENTON

FENTON
How now, good woman? how dost thou?

MISTRESS QUICKLY
The better that it pleases your good worship to ask.

FENTON
What news? how does pretty Mistress Anne?

MISTRESS QUICKLY
In truth, sir, and she is pretty, and honest, and gentle; and one that is your friend, I can tell you that by the way; I praise heaven for it.

FENTON
Shall I do any good, thinkest thou? shall I not lose my suit?

MISTRESS QUICKLY
Troth, sir, all is in his hands above: but notwithstanding, Master Fenton, I'll be sworn on a book, she loves you. Have not your worship a wart above your eye?

FENTON
Yes, marry, have I; what of that?

MISTRESS QUICKLY
Well, thereby hangs a tale: good faith, it is such another Nan; but, I detest, an honest maid as ever broke bread: we had an hour's talk of that wart. I shall never laugh but in that maid's company! But indeed she is given too much to allicholy and musing: but for you--well, go to.

FENTON
Well, I shall see her to-day. Hold, there's money for thee; let me have thy voice in my behalf: if thou seest her before me, commend me.

MISTRESS QUICKLY
Will I? i'faith, that we will; and I will tell your worship more of the wart the next time we have confidence; and of other wooers.

Who's that, I wonder! Come up to the door, please.

What's going on, good woman? How are you?

I'm all the better for a good man like you enquiring.

What's the news? How is pretty Mistress Anne?

To tell the truth, sir, she is pretty, and honest, and gentle; and by the way I can tell you that she likes you; I praise heaven for it.

Do you think I will get anywhere? Won't my proposal be turned down?

To tell you the truth, sir, it's all in God's hands: but nevertheless, Master Fenton, I'll swear on the Bible, she loves you. Doesn't your worship have a wart above his eye?

I certainly have; what about it?

Well, there's a story attached to that: my goodness, she is such a woman, but I must say, as honest a girl as ever broke bread: we talked for an hour about that wart. That girl is the only one who can make me laugh! But she is too inclined to depression and brooding: except when thinking of you–well, there you go.

Well, I shall see her today. Wait, here's money for you; please speak on my behalf: if you see her before I do, praise me.

Will I? I certainly shall; and I will tell your worship more of what she says about the wart the next time we confer; and I'll tell you about her other suitors.

FENTON
Well, farewell; I am in great haste now.

Good, goodbye; I'm in a great hurry now.

MISTRESS QUICKLY

Farewell to your worship.

Farewell to your worship.

Exit FENTON

Truly, an honest gentleman: but Anne loves him
not;
for I know Anne's mind as well as another does. Out
upon't! what have I forgot?

*He's truly a good gentleman: but Anne does not
love him;
I know Anne's mind as well as anybody else.
Damnation! What have I forgotten?*

Exit

Act 2

SCENE I. Before PAGE'S house.

Enter MISTRESS PAGE, with a letter

MISTRESS PAGE
What, have I scaped love-letters in the holiday-
time of my beauty, and am I now a subject for
them?
Let me see.

Reads
'Ask me no reason why I love you; for though
Love use Reason for his physician, he admits him
not for his counsellor. You are not young, no more
am I; go to then, there's sympathy: you are merry,
so am I; ha, ha! then there's more sympathy: you
love sack, and so do I; would you desire better
sympathy? Let it suffice thee, Mistress Page,--at
the least, if the love of soldier can suffice,--
that I love thee. I will not say, pity me; 'tis
not a soldier-like phrase: but I say, love me. By me,
Thine own true knight,
By day or night,
Or any kind of light,
With all his might
For thee to fight, JOHN FALSTAFF'
What a Herod of Jewry is this! O wicked
world! One that is well-nigh worn to pieces with
age to show himself a young gallant! What an
unweighed behavior hath this Flemish drunkard
picked--with the devil's name!--out of my
conversation, that he dares in this manner assay me?
Why, he hath not been thrice in my company! What
should I say to him? I was then frugal of my
mirth: Heaven forgive me! Why, I'll exhibit a bill
in the parliament for the putting down of men. How
shall I be revenged on him? for revenged I will be,
as sure as his guts are made of puddings.

Enter MISTRESS FORD

MISTRESS FORD
Mistress Page! trust me, I was going to your house.

MISTRESS PAGE
And, trust me, I was coming to you. You look very
ill.

MISTRESS FORD

What, I didn't get any love letters when my beauty was at its height, and I get them now? Let's have a look.

'Don't ask me why I love you, for although love uses reason as a guide, it does not use it as a counsellor. You are not young, neither am I; well then, there's a bond. You are jolly, so am I; well then, there's another bond. You love sherry, so do I; who could ask for a more perfect match? Let it be enough for you, Mistress Page–at least, if the love of a soldier is good enough–that I love you. I won't ask you to pity me–that's not something soldiers say–but I say, love me. Believe me to be, your own true knight, by day or night, or any kind of light, who will with all his might for you fight, John Falstaff.'
What Jewish Herod is this? What a wicked world: someone who is falling apart with age acts like a young buck! What unbalanced impression has this Flemish drunkard got– in the name of the devil–from my conversation, that he thinks he can make advances to me like this? Why, he hasn't met me three times! What did he think I would say to him? I was most reserved. Heaven forgive me! Why, I'll put forward a bill in Parliament to have men suppressed. How shall I retaliate? For I will retaliate, as sure as he has sausages for guts.

Mistress Page! Believe me, I was just going to your house.

And, believe me, I was just coming to you. You look very ill.

Nay, I'll ne'er believe that; I have to show to the contrary.

No, I won't believe that; I can show you different.

MISTRESS PAGE
Faith, but you do, in my mind.

Well you do, to my mind.

MISTRESS FORD
Well, I do then; yet I say I could show you to the contrary. O Mistress Page, give me some counsel!

Alright then, I do; but I still say I could prove the opposite. Oh Mistress Page, give me some advice!

MISTRESS PAGE
What's the matter, woman?

What's the matter, woman?

MISTRESS FORD
O woman, if it were not for one trifling respect, I could come to such honour!

Oh woman, if it wasn't for just one small thing, I could be so honoured!

MISTRESS PAGE
Hang the trifle, woman! take the honour. What is it? dispense with trifles; what is it?

Forget the small thing, woman! Take the honour. What is it? Forget the small things; what is it?

MISTRESS FORD
If I would but go to hell for an eternal moment or so,
I could be knighted.

*If I would only do something which could get me sent to hell,
I could be knighted.*

MISTRESS PAGE
What? thou liest! Sir Alice Ford! These knights will hack; and so thou shouldst not alter the article of thy gentry.

What? You lie! Sir Alice Ford! These knights are sluts; so you should never change your title.

MISTRESS FORD
We burn daylight: here, read, read; perceive how I might be knighted. I shall think the worse of fat men, as long as I have an eye to make difference of men's liking: and yet he would not swear; praised women's modesty; and gave such orderly and well-behaved reproof to all uncomeliness, that I would have sworn his disposition would have gone to
the truth of his words; but they do no more adhere and keep place together than the Hundredth Psalm to
the tune of 'Green Sleeves.' What tempest, I trow, threw this whale, with so many tuns of oil in his belly, ashore at Windsor? How shall I be revenged on him? I think the best way were to entertain him with hope, till the wicked fire of lust have melted him in his own grease. Did you ever hear the like?

*We are wasting time: here, read this; see how I might be knighted. I shall never like fat men, for as long as I have eyes to judge between men's looks: and yet he did not swear; praised women's modesty; and gave such a reasonable and sensible criticism of all improper behaviour, I would have sworn that his personality must match the truth of his words; but they are no better suited to each other than the hundredth Psalm is to the tune of 'Greensleeves'. What storm, I wonder, cast this whale, with so many barrels of oil in his belly, ashore at Windsor? How shall I take my retaliation?
I think the best way would be to lead him on until the wicked fire of lust has made him dissolve in his own fat. Did you ever hear anything like it?*

MISTRESS PAGE

Letter for letter, but that the name of Page and
Ford differs! To thy great comfort in this mystery
of ill opinions, here's the twin-brother of thy
letter: but let thine inherit first; for, I
protest, mine never shall. I warrant he hath a
thousand of these letters, writ with blank space for
different names--sure, more,--and these are of the
second edition: he will print them, out of doubt;
for he cares not what he puts into the press, when
he would put us two. I had rather be a giantess,
and lie under Mount Pelion. Well, I will find you
twenty lascivious turtles ere one chaste man.

*Exactly like it, except that the name of Page and
Ford is different! If you want to see a solution to
this mystery of his poor opinion, here's the twin
brother of your letter: but your one can inherit
what's on offer; for, I swear, mine never will. I don't
doubt he has a thousand of these letters, with a
blank space left for different names–in fact, I should
think that these are from his second edition: he
doubtless has them printed; he obviously doesn't
care who he sends them to, when he tries it on with
us. I would rather be a giant, crushed under Mount
Pelion. Well, you will find twenty unfaithful
turtledoves before you find a single pure man.*

MISTRESS FORD

Why, this is the very same; the very hand, the very
words. What doth he think of us?

*Why, this is exactly the same; the same handwriting,
the same words. Who does he think we are?*

MISTRESS PAGE

Nay, I know not: it makes me almost ready to
wrangle with mine own honesty. I'll entertain
myself like one that I am not acquainted withal;
for, sure, unless he know some strain in me, that I
know not myself, he would never have boarded me
in this fury.

*I've no idea: it almost makes me start to question
my own virtue. I look upon myself
as if I am a stranger;
for, unless he knows something about me I don't,
he would never have boarded me with this attack.*

MISTRESS FORD

'Boarding,' call you it? I'll be sure to keep him
above deck.

*'Boarding,' you call it? I'll make sure he keeps
above the deck.*

MISTRESS PAGE

So will I: if he come under my hatches, I'll never
to sea again. Let's be revenged on him: let's
appoint him a meeting; give him a show of comfort
in
his suit and lead him on with a fine-baited delay,
till he hath pawned his horses to mine host of the
Garter.

*So will I: if he ever invaded me, that would be
the end of my travels. Let's get our revenge on him:
let's arrange a meeting; we'll make him think that
he has a chance with us and lead him on with
tantalising promises,
until he has pawned his horses to the landlord of the
Garter.*

MISTRESS FORD

Nay, I will consent to act any villany against him,
that may not sully the chariness of our honesty. O,
that my husband saw this letter! it would give
eternal food to his jealousy.

*Absolutely, I will participate in any tricks against
him, as long as it does not produce any stain on our
absolute honesty. Oh, if my husband saw this letter!
It would give him reasons to be jealous for ever.*

MISTRESS PAGE

Why, look where he comes; and my good man too:
he's
as far from jealousy as I am from giving him cause;

*Why, look, he's coming; and my husband too: he's
as unlikely to be jealous as I am to give him a
reason to be;*

and that I hope is an unmeasurable distance.

and I know that is unthinkable.

MISTRESS FORD
You are the happier woman.

You're better off than me then.

MISTRESS PAGE
Let's consult together against this greasy knight.
Come hither.

Let's plot together against this greasy knight.
Come with me.

They retire

Enter FORD with PISTOL, and PAGE with NYM

FORD
Well, I hope it be not so.

Well, I hope this is not true.

PISTOL
Hope is a curtal dog in some affairs:
Sir John affects thy wife.

Hope is a useless thing in some matters:
Sir John fancies your wife.

FORD
Why, sir, my wife is not young.

Why, sir, my wife is not young.

PISTOL
He woos both high and low, both rich and poor,
Both young and old, one with another, Ford;
He loves the gallimaufry: Ford, perpend.

He woos both high and low, both rich and poor,
both young and old, all at the same time, Ford;
he loves the mixture: Ford, think about this.

FORD
Love my wife!

He loves my wife!

PISTOL
With liver burning hot. Prevent, or go thou,
Like Sir Actaeon he, with Ringwood at thy heels:
O, odious is the name!

With a burning passion. Block him or you'll be like
Actaeon, torn apart by his own dogs:
was a horrible name it is!

FORD
What name, sir?

What name, sir?

PISTOL
The horn, I say. Farewell.
Take heed, have open eye, for thieves do foot by
night:
Take heed, ere summer comes or cuckoo-birds do
sing.
Away, Sir Corporal Nym!
Believe it, Page; he speaks sense.

The name of cuckold, I say. Goodbye.
Be careful, keep your eyes open, for thieves come in
the night:
be careful, before summer comes and you find a
cuckoo in your nest.
Come on, Sir Corporal Nym!
Believe it, Page; he's telling you the truth.

Exit

FORD
[Aside] I will be patient; I will find out this.

I will bide my time; I will find out about this.

NYM
[To PAGE] And this is true; I like not the humour
of lying. He hath wronged me in some humours: I
should have borne the humoured letter to her; but I
have a sword and it shall bite upon my necessity.
He loves your wife; there's the short and the long.
My name is Corporal Nym; I speak and I avouch;
'tis
true: my name is Nym and Falstaff loves your wife.
Adieu. I love not the humour of bread and cheese,
and there's the humour of it. Adieu.

And it's all true; I do not like
to lie. He has done me wrong: I
should have carried that letter to her; but I
have a sword and I'm not afraid to use it.
He loves your wife; that's the long and the short of
it. My name is Corporal Nym; I swear that what I
tell you
is true: my name is Nym, and Falstaff loves your
wife. Goodbye. I'm not going to live on bread and
cheese. Goodbye.

Exit

PAGE
'The humour of it,' quoth a'! here's a fellow
frights English out of his wits.

'The humour of it,' he says! Here's a fellow
who scares English out of its wits.

**[Editor's note: in the speech by Nym, 'humour' is used in multiple ways which it is impossible to
convey by replacing it with a single modern word, so Page's reference to it here should be noted in the
context of the original]**

FORD
I will seek out Falstaff.

I will go and find Falstaff.

PAGE
I never heard such a drawling, affecting rogue.

I never heard such a drawling, affected scoundrel.

FORD
If I do find it: well.

If I do find him, we shall see what happens.

PAGE
I will not believe such a Cataian, though the priest
o' the town commended him for a true man.

I will never believe such a liar, even if the priest
of the town said that he was honest.

FORD
'Twas a good sensible fellow: well.

That makes sense: well well.

PAGE
How now, Meg!

Hello there, Meg!

MISTRESS PAGE and MISTRESS FORD come forward

MISTRESS PAGE
Whither go you, George? Hark you.

Where are you going, George? Tell me.

MISTRESS FORD

How now, sweet Frank! why art thou melancholy?

Hello there, sweet Frank! Why do you look so sad?

FORD
I melancholy! I am not melancholy. Get you home,
go.

Me sad! I am not sad. You go home.

MISTRESS FORD
Faith, thou hast some crotchets in thy head. Now,
will you go, Mistress Page?

*You seem to have some daft ideas.
Will you come, Mistress Page?*

MISTRESS PAGE
Have with you. You'll come to dinner, George.

*I'll come with you. You be back in time for dinner,
George.*

Aside to MISTRESS FORD
Look who comes yonder: she shall be our
messenger
to this paltry knight.

*Look who's coming: she shall be our messenger
to this worthless knight.*

MISTRESS FORD
[Aside to MISTRESS PAGE] Trust me, I thought
on her:
she'll fit it.

*Believe me, I'd already thought of her:
she's just right for the job.*

Enter MISTRESS QUICKLY

MISTRESS PAGE
You are come to see my daughter Anne?

Have you come to see my daughter Anne?

MISTRESS QUICKLY
Ay, forsooth; and, I pray, how does good Mistress
Anne?

*Indeed I have; and, may I ask, how is good Mistress
Anne?*

MISTRESS PAGE
Go in with us and see: we have an hour's talk with
you.

*Come in with us and see for yourself: we have a lot
to talk to you about.*

PAGE
How now, Master Ford!

Hello there, Master Ford!

FORD
You heard what this knave told me, did you not?

You heard what this scoundrel told me, didn't you?

PAGE
Yes: and you heard what the other told me?

Yes: and you heard what the other one told me?

FORD
Do you think there is truth in them?

Do you think they are truthful?

PAGE
Hang 'em, slaves! I do not think the knight would

Damn them, the scoundrels! I don't think the knight

offer it: but these that accuse him in his intent towards our wives are a yoke of his discarded men; very rogues, now they be out of service.

FORD
Were they his men?

PAGE
Marry, were they.

FORD
I like it never the better for that. Does he lie at the Garter?

PAGE
Ay, marry, does he. If he should intend this voyage towards my wife, I would turn her loose to him; and what he gets more of her than sharp words, let it lie on my head.

FORD
I do not misdoubt my wife; but I would be loath to turn them together. A man may be too confident: I would have nothing lie on my head: I cannot be thus satisfied.

PAGE
Look where my ranting host of the Garter comes: there is either liquor in his pate or money in his purse when he looks so merrily.

Enter Host
How now, mine host!

Host
How now, bully-rook! thou'rt a gentleman. Cavaleiro-justice, I say!

Enter SHALLOW

SHALLOW
I follow, mine host, I follow. Good even and twenty, good Master Page! Master Page, will you go
with us? we have sport in hand.

Host
Tell him, cavaleiro-justice; tell him, bully-rook.

SHALLOW

---

would try this on: these men who accuse him of having designs on our wives are both men who've been sacked by him; they are absolute rascals, now they're not in his employ.

Were they his men?

They certainly were.

I don't like it any better for that. Is he lodging at the Garter?

Yes he is. If he intends to make this attempt on my wife, I'm inclined to turn her loose on him; if he gets anything more from her than harsh words, then on my own head be it.

I don't distrust my wife; but I wouldn't like to put them together. A man can be overconfident: I don't want any blame on my head: I wouldn't be happy with that.

Here comes the landlord of the Garter, chuntering away: he's either got booze in his belly or money in his purse, he looks so happy.

What's up, mine host!

Hello there, my fine fellow! You are a gentleman. A gallant lad, I say!

*I'm with you, mine host, I'm with you. Good day twenty times over, good Master Page! Master Page, will you
come with us? We've got some fun going.*

Tell him about it, gallant fellow; tell him about it, my dear chap.

Sir, there is a fray to be fought between Sir Hugh
the Welsh priest and Caius the French doctor.

FORD
Good mine host o' the Garter, a word with you.

Drawing him aside

Host
What sayest thou, my bully-rook?

SHALLOW
[To PAGE] Will you go with us to behold it? My
merry host hath had the measuring of their
weapons;
and, I think, hath appointed them contrary places;
for, believe me, I hear the parson is no jester.
Hark, I will tell you what our sport shall be.

They converse apart

Host
Hast thou no suit against my knight, my
guest-cavaleire?

FORD
None, I protest: but I'll give you a pottle of
burnt sack to give me recourse to him and tell him
my name is Brook; only for a jest.

Host
My hand, bully; thou shalt have egress and regress;
--said I well?--and thy name shall be Brook. It is
a merry knight. Will you go, An-heires?

SHALLOW
Have with you, mine host.

PAGE
I have heard the Frenchman hath good skill in
his rapier.

SHALLOW
Tut, sir, I could have told you more. In these times
you stand on distance, your passes, stoccadoes, and
I know not what: 'tis the heart, Master Page; 'tis
here, 'tis here. I have seen the time, with my long
sword I would have made you four tall fellows skip
like rats.

*Sir, there is going to be a duel between Sir Hugh
the Welsh priest and Caius the French doctor.*

*My dear landlord of the Garter, may I have a word
with you?*

What is it you want, old chap?

*Will you come with us to see it? My
jolly host has examined their weapons;
I think he has also set the place for the fight;
for, believe me, I hear the parson is very much in
earnest.
Listen, I'll tell you what fun we'll have.*

*You haven't any quarrel with my knight,
my brave guest?*

*None, I assure you: but I'll give you half a gallon of
sweet sherry to let me in to see him and tell him
my name is Brook; just for a joke.*

*Shake on it, lad; I'll let you come and go freely;
--was that a good phrase?--and you shall be called
Brook. He is
a jolly knight. Will you come along, gentleman?*

I'm with you, mine host.

*I've heard the Frenchman is pretty handy with
his sword.*

*Tut, sir, I could do better than him. These days
they toe the line, they make all sorts of fancy moves:
good fighting comes from the heart, Master Page; it
is in here, here. I can remember the days when I
could have made you four big fellows jump like rats
with my long sword.*

Host

Here, boys, here, here! shall we wag?

Here, boys, come on, come on! Shall we go in?

PAGE

Have with you. I would rather hear them scold than fight.

I'll come with you. I would rather hear them arguing than fight.

Exeunt Host, SHALLOW, and PAGE

FORD

Though Page be a secure fool, an stands so firmly on his wife's frailty, yet I cannot put off my opinion so easily: she was in his company at Page's house; and what they made there, I know not. Well, I will look further into't: and I have a disguise to sound Falstaff. If I find her honest, I lose not my labour; if she be otherwise, 'tis labour well bestowed.

Although Page is foolishly overconfident, and puts so much faith in his wife's weakness, I can't be quite so confident; she was with him at Page's house; and what they got up to there, I don't know. Well, I will investigate it further: I have a plan by which I shall quiz Falstaff. If I find she's faithful, that won't be a waste of time; if she is not, it will be time well spent.

Exit

SCENE II. A room in the Garter Inn.

Enter FALSTAFF and PISTOL

FALSTAFF
I will not lend thee a penny.

PISTOL
Why, then the world's mine oyster,
Which I with sword will open.

FALSTAFF
Not a penny. I have been content, sir, you should
lay my countenance to pawn; I have grated upon my
good friends for three reprieves for you and your
coach-fellow Nym; or else you had looked through
the grate, like a geminy of baboons. I am damned in
hell for swearing to gentlemen my friends, you were
good soldiers and tall fellows; and when Mistress
Bridget lost the handle of her fan, I took't upon
mine honour thou hadst it not.

PISTOL
Didst not thou share? hadst thou not fifteen pence?

FALSTAFF
Reason, you rogue, reason: thinkest thou I'll
endanger my soul gratis? At a word, hang no more
about me, I am no gibbet for you. Go. A short knife
and a throng! To your manor of Pickt-hatch! Go.
You'll not bear a letter for me, you rogue! you
stand upon your honour! Why, thou unconfinable
baseness, it is as much as I can do to keep the
terms of my honour precise: I, I, I myself
sometimes, leaving the fear of God on the left hand
and hiding mine honour in my necessity, am fain to
shuffle, to hedge and to lurch; and yet you, rogue,
will ensconce your rags, your cat-a-mountain
looks, your red-lattice phrases, and your
bold-beating oaths, under the shelter of your
honour! You will not do it, you!

PISTOL
I do relent: what would thou more of man?

Enter ROBIN

ROBIN
Sir, here's a woman would speak with you.

I won't lend you a penny.

*Well then, I shall have to get my living
with my sword.*

*Not a penny. I've been happy, sir, to let you
borrow using my good name; three times I have
pestered my friends to get reprieves for you and
your fellow traveller Nym; otherwise you would be
looking through the bars of a cage, like a pair of
baboons. I will go to hell for swearing to these
gentlemen, my friends, that you were
good soldiers and brave fellows; and when Mistress
Bridget lost her fan holder, I gave my word of
honour that you didn't have it.*

*Didn't you get a share of the profits? Didn't we give
you fifteen pence?*

*Wasn't that deserved, you scoundrel? Do you think
I'll risk my soul for nothing? I'm telling you, don't
try to hang anything else on me; I am not your
scaffold. Go and pick pockets in a crowd, off to the
slums! You won't carry a letter for me, you
scoundrel? You say
it's a question of honour? Why, you infinite
lowness, it's as much as I can do to keep
my own honour: even I sometimes have to
put away my fear of heaven and make my needs
more important than my honour; I have had to
cheat, scam and steal; and yet you, you scoundrel,
protect your rags, your cat's whiskers, your bar
room speech and your grating oaths under the
shield of honour?*

I give in: what more can you ask for?

Sir, there's a woman here who wants to speak to

FALSTAFF
Let her approach.

Enter MISTRESS QUICKLY

MISTRESS QUICKLY
Give your worship good morrow.

FALSTAFF
Good morrow, good wife.

MISTRESS QUICKLY
Not so, an't please your worship.

FALSTAFF
Good maid, then.

MISTRESS QUICKLY
I'll be sworn,
As my mother was, the first hour I was born.

FALSTAFF
I do believe the swearer. What with me?

MISTRESS QUICKLY
Shall I vouchsafe your worship a word or two?

FALSTAFF
Two thousand, fair woman: and I'll vouchsafe thee
the hearing.

MISTRESS QUICKLY
There is one Mistress Ford, sir:--I pray, come a
little nearer this ways:--I myself dwell with master
Doctor Caius,--

FALSTAFF
Well, on: Mistress Ford, you say,--

MISTRESS QUICKLY
Your worship says very true: I pray your worship,
come a little nearer this ways.

FALSTAFF
I warrant thee, nobody hears; mine own people,
mine
own people.

MISTRESS QUICKLY

you.

Send her in.

Good day to your worship.

Good day, good madam.

Not madam, if your worship doesn't mind.

Good miss, then.

*I'll swear that I'm
as much of a maid as my mother was, the day I was
born.*

I'll believe you. What can I do for you?

Can I give your worship a word or two?

*Two thousand, fair woman: and I will lend you
my ear.*

*There is a woman called Mistress Ford, sir–please,
come a little closer:–I myself live with master
Doctor Caius.*

Right, move on: Mistress Ford, you say–

*That's right, your worship: please your worship,
come a little closer.*

*I promise you, nobody is listening; these are all
my own people.*

Are they so? God bless them and make them his servants!

Are they indeed? May God bless them and take them into heaven!

FALSTAFF
Well, Mistress Ford; what of her?

Now then, Mistress Ford; what about her?

MISTRESS QUICKLY
Why, sir, she's a good creature. Lord Lord! your worship's a wanton! Well, heaven forgive you and all
of us, I pray!

Well, sir, she is a good woman. Good Lord! Your worship is a randy devil! Well, may heaven forgive you
and forgive all of us, I hope!

FALSTAFF
Mistress Ford; come, Mistress Ford,--

Mistress Ford; come on, about Mistress Ford—

MISTRESS QUICKLY
Marry, this is the short and the long of it; you have brought her into such a canaries as 'tis wonderful. The best courtier of them all, when the court lay at Windsor, could never have brought her to such a canary. Yet there has been knights, and lords, and gentlemen, with their coaches, I warrant you, coach after coach, letter after letter, gift after gift; smelling so sweetly, all musk, and so rushling, I warrant you, in silk and gold; and in such alligant terms; and in such wine and sugar of the best and the fairest, that would have won any woman's heart; and, I warrant you, they could never get an eye-wink of her: I had myself twenty angels given me this morning; but I defy all angels, in any such sort, as they say, but in the way of honesty: and, I warrant you, they could never get her so much as sip on a cup with the proudest of them all: and yet there has been earls, nay, which is more, pensioners; but, I warrant you, all is one with her.

Well, this is the long and the short of it; you have thrown her all into confusion.
The best of all the courtiers, when the court was at Windsor, could never have got her in such a state. There were knights, lords, and gentlemen, in their coaches—I promise you, coach after coach, letter after letter, gift after gift—smelling so sweetly, all perfumed, and rustling, I assure you, with silk and cloth of gold, speaking in such elegant terms, with such honeyed words that they would have won any woman's heart; and, I promise you, they could never get so much as a wink out of her: I was given twenty gold coins this morning; not that I would let that sway me of course; and I promise you, they could never get her to have so much
as a drink with them, even the greatest of them, and there have been
earls, and even better, pensioners, but
I promise you, they're all the same to her.

FALSTAFF
But what says she to me? be brief, my good she-Mercury.

But what does she want to say to me? Be quick, my good female Mercury.

MISTRESS QUICKLY
Marry, she hath received your letter, for the which she thanks you a thousand times; and she gives you to notify that her husband will be absence from his house between ten and eleven.

Well, she got your letter, for which she sends you a thousand thanks; and she wants you to know that her husband will not be in his house between ten and eleven.

FALSTAFF
Ten and eleven?

Ten and eleven?

MISTRESS QUICKLY

Ay, forsooth; and then you may come and see the picture, she says, that you wot of: Master Ford, her husband, will be from home. Alas! the sweet woman leads an ill life with him: he's a very jealousy man: she leads a very frampold life with him, good heart.

FALSTAFF

Ten and eleven. Woman, commend me to her; I will not fail her.

MISTRESS QUICKLY

Why, you say well. But I have another messenger to your worship. Mistress Page hath her hearty commendations to you too: and let me tell you in your ear, she's as fartuous a civil modest wife, and one, I tell you, that will not miss you morning nor evening prayer, as any is in Windsor, whoe'er be the other: and she bade me tell your worship that her husband is seldom from home; but she hopes there will come a time. I never knew a woman so dote upon
a man: surely I think you have charms, la; yes, in truth.

FALSTAFF

Not I, I assure thee: setting the attractions of my good parts aside I have no other charms.

MISTRESS QUICKLY

Blessing on your heart for't!

FALSTAFF

But, I pray thee, tell me this: has Ford's wife and Page's wife acquainted each other how they love me?

MISTRESS QUICKLY

That were a jest indeed! they have not so little grace, I hope: that were a trick indeed! but Mistress Page would desire you to send her your little page, of all loves: her husband has a marvellous infection to the little page; and truly Master Page is an honest man. Never a wife in Windsor leads a better life than she does: do what she will, say what she will, take all, pay all, go to bed when she list, rise when she list, all is as she will: and truly she deserves it; for if there be a kind woman in Windsor, she is one. You must

Yes, indeed; and at that time you can come and see the picture that she says you know about: Master Ford, her husband, will be away. Alas! The sweet woman has a very poor life with him: he's a very jealous man: she has a very turbulent life with him, the good lady.

Ten and eleven. Woman, give her my compliments; I will not fail her.

Well said. But I have another message for your worship: Mistress Page has also sent her warm wishes to you; and let me whisper to you, she's as good, polite and modest a wife, who I can tell you never misses morning or evening prayers, as any in Windsor, whomever you compare her with; and she told me to tell your worship that her husband is not often away, but she hopes that there will be an opportunity. I never knew a woman to be so fascinated by man; it's as if you have a magic charm;
I really think you must have.

I don't, I can promise you: apart from my good looks and good qualities I have no other magic.

Bless you for it!

But, please, could you tell me this: have Ford's wife and
Page's wife told each other how they love me?

That would be a good joke! I don't think they would be so unsubtle; goodness that would be a joke! But Mistress Page would like you to send her your young servant, for the sake of love: her husband is very keen on the little chap; and it's a fact that Master Page is an honest man. There is no wife in Windsor who has a better lifestyle than her: she does whatever she wants, says what she wants, gets whatever she wants, has it paid for, goes to bed when she wants, gets up when she wants, everything is how she wants it: and she really does deserve it;

send her your page; no remedy.

for if there is a single good woman in Windsor, she's one. You must send her your page, there is no alternative.

FALSTAFF
Why, I will.

Well, I will.

MISTRESS QUICKLY
Nay, but do so, then: and, look you, he may come
and
go between you both; and in any case have a
nay-word, that you may know one another's mind,
and
the boy never need to understand any thing; for
'tis not good that children should know any
wickedness: old folks, you know, have discretion,
as they say, and know the world.

Well, do so, then: and, you see, he can be your go-between; and so you should have a password, so that you can know what the other one is thinking, and the boy will never understand a word; because it is not good for children to know of any wickedness: older people, as you know, can be discreet, as they have knowledge of the world.

FALSTAFF
Fare thee well: commend me to them both: there's
my purse; I am yet thy debtor. Boy, go along with
this woman.

Goodbye: give my regards to both of them: here's my purse; I am still in your debt. Boy, go with this woman.

Exeunt MISTRESS QUICKLY and ROBIN

This news distracts me!

PISTOL
This punk is one of Cupid's carriers:
Clap on more sails; pursue; up with your fights:
Give fire: she is my prize, or ocean whelm them all!

This slut is one of Cupid's ships: put on more sail; chase her; put up your shields: fire away: she is my trophy, or let the ocean swallow them all up!

Exit

FALSTAFF
Sayest thou so, old Jack? go thy ways; I'll make
more of thy old body than I have done. Will they
yet look after thee? Wilt thou, after the expense
of so much money, be now a gainer? Good body, I
thank thee. Let them say 'tis grossly done; so it be
fairly done, no matter.

So that's what the old Falstaff would say, is it? On your way. I'll make better use of your old body than you have. Will they now look after you? Will you, after laying out so much money, make a profit? My good body, I thank you. They can say that it is gross, but who cares as long as it gets results.

Enter BARDOLPH

BARDOLPH
Sir John, there's one Master Brook below would
fain
speak with you, and be acquainted with you; and
hath
sent your worship a morning's draught of sack.

Sir John, there's a Master Brook downstairs who wants to meet you and speak to you; he has sent your worship a morning drink of sherry.

FALSTAFF
Brook is his name?

He's called Brook?

BARDOLPH
Ay, sir.

Yes, sir.

FALSTAFF
Call him in.

Send him in.

Exit BARDOLPH

Such Brooks are welcome to me, that o'erflow such liquor. Ah, ha! Mistress Ford and Mistress Page have I encompassed you? go to; via!

I'll always welcome a Brook, if it's running with such liquor. Aha! Mistress Ford and Mistress Page, have I snared you? Come on then, let's hurry up!

Re-enter BARDOLPH, with FORD disguised

FORD
Bless you, sir!

Bless you, sir!

FALSTAFF
And you, sir! Would you speak with me?

And you, sir! You want to talk to me?

FORD
I make bold to press with so little preparation upon you.

If I might be so bold as to impose on you with so little introduction.

FALSTAFF
You're welcome. What's your will? Give us leave, drawer.

You're welcome. What is it you want? Leave us alone, barman.

Exit BARDOLPH

FORD
Sir, I am a gentleman that have spent much; my name is Brook.

Sir, I am a gentleman who has spent much; my name is Brook.

FALSTAFF
Good Master Brook, I desire more acquaintance of you.

Good Master Brook, I would like to know you better.

FORD
Good Sir John, I sue for yours: not to charge you; for I must let you understand I think myself in better plight for a lender than you are: the which hath something embolden'd me to this unseasoned intrusion; for they say, if money go before, all ways do lie open.

Good Sir John, I'd like to know you: not to sponge off you,
for I must tell you that I am in a better position to lend money than you are: that's why I'm cheeky enough to make this uninvited intrusion; they do say that money opens all doors.

FALSTAFF

Money is a good soldier, sir, and will on.

Money is a good soldier, sir, and marches on.

FORD
Troth, and I have a bag of money here troubles me:
if you will help to bear it, Sir John, take all, or
half, for easing me of the carriage.

Well I tell you, I have a bag of money here which is weighing me down: if you will help me to carry it, Sir John, take it all, or half, as payment for lifting the weight off me.

FALSTAFF
Sir, I know not how I may deserve to be your
porter.

Sir, I don't know why you would choose me as your porter.

FORD
I will tell you, sir, if you will give me the hearing.

I will tell you, sir, if you will allow me.

FALSTAFF
Speak, good Master Brook: I shall be glad to be
your servant.

Speak, good Master Brook: I will be glad to be your servant.

FORD
Sir, I hear you are a scholar,--I will be brief
with you,--and you have been a man long known to
me,
though I had never so good means, as desire, to
make
myself acquainted with you. I shall discover a
thing to you, wherein I must very much lay open
mine
own imperfection: but, good Sir John, as you have
one eye upon my follies, as you hear them unfolded,
turn another into the register of your own; that I
may pass with a reproof the easier, sith you
yourself know how easy it is to be such an offender.

Sir, I hear that you are a scholar–I'll be as quick as I can–and I have known about you for a long time, although my means never matched my desire to make your acquaintance. I shall reveal something to you by which I will very much show my own faults: but, good Sir John, as you hear about my mistakes, bear in mind the list of your own; that will make you more indulgent towards me, since you yourself know how easy it is to slip up.

FALSTAFF
Very well, sir; proceed.

Very good, sir; carry on.

FORD
There is a gentlewoman in this town; her husband's
name is Ford.

There is a gentlewoman in this town; her husband's name is Ford.

FALSTAFF
Well, sir.

Go on, sir.

FORD
I have long loved her, and, I protest to you,
bestowed much on her; followed her with a doting
observance; engrossed opportunities to meet her;
fee'd every slight occasion that could but niggardly
give me sight of her; not only bought many presents
to give her, but have given largely to many to know

I have loved her for a long time, and, I must tell you, have given her many things; paid attention to her every need; taken every opportunity to meet her; paid for any opportunity which might just give me a glimpse of her; not only bought many presents for her, but have paid a lot to other people to know

what she would have given; briefly, I have pursued her as love hath pursued me; which hath been on the wing of all occasions. But whatsoever I have merited, either in my mind or, in my means, meed, I am sure, I have received none; unless experience be a jewel that I have purchased at an infinite rate, and that hath taught me to say this:
'Love like a shadow flies when substance love pursues;
Pursuing that that flies, and flying what pursues.'

FALSTAFF
Have you received no promise of satisfaction at her hands?

FORD
Never.

FALSTAFF
Have you importuned her to such a purpose?

FORD
Never.

FALSTAFF
Of what quality was your love, then?

FORD
Like a fair house built on another man's ground; so that I have lost my edifice by mistaking the place where I erected it.

FALSTAFF
To what purpose have you unfolded this to me?

FORD
When I have told you that, I have told you all. Some say, that though she appear honest to me, yet in
other places she enlargeth her mirth so far that there is shrewd construction made of her. Now, Sir John, here is the heart of my purpose: you are a gentleman of excellent breeding, admirable discourse, of great admittance, authentic in your place and person, generally allowed for your many war-like, court-like, and learned preparations.

FALSTAFF
O, sir!

---

*what sort of presents she would like; in short, I have chased her as love chased me; it was that which always spurred me on. But whatever I deserved, either for myself or my gifts, I have definitely got no reward; unless experience is a jewel, that I have bought for an infinite price and that has taught me to say this:
Love flies away like a shadow when money chases it,
it runs away and takes at the same time.*

Hasn't she promised to give you what you want?

Never.

Have you ever suggested such a thing to her?

Never.

What was your love like, then?

Like a good house built on somebody else's land; so I have lost my building by putting it up in the wrong place.

And why are you telling me this?

Once I have explained that, I've told you everything. Some say that although she seems pure with me, with others she lets her passions have free rein, and there is plenty to be got from her. Now, Sir John, this is the heart of the matter: you are a gentleman of excellent breeding, admirable speech, you are welcomed everywhere, you are a very genuine person, universally admired for all your soldierly, courtly and scholarly virtues.

Oh, sir!

FORD

Believe it, for you know it. There is money; spend it, spend it; spend more; spend all I have; only give me so much of your time in exchange of it, as to lay an amiable siege to the honesty of this Ford's wife: use your art of wooing; win her to consent to you: if any man may, you may as soon as any.

You know it's true. Here is some money; spend it, spend it; spend more; spend everything I have; all I ask in exchange is enough of your time to make a good attack on the honesty of Ford's wife: use your seductive arts; get her to give in to you: if any man can do it it's you.

FALSTAFF

Would it apply well to the vehemency of your affection, that I should win what you would enjoy? Methinks you prescribe to yourself very preposterously.

What good would it do your love if I got what you want? I don't think you're doing yourself any favours.

FORD

O, understand my drift. She dwells so securely on the excellency of her honour, that the folly of my soul dares not present itself: she is too bright to be looked against. Now, could I could come to her with any detection in my hand, my desires had instance and argument to commend themselves: I could drive her then from the ward of her purity, her reputation, her marriage-vow, and a thousand other her defences, which now are too too strongly embattled against me. What say you to't, Sir John?

Oh, understand my plan. She is so concerned with upholding her virtue that I dare not show her my foolish desires: she is too good for me to try that. Now, if I could approach her with evidence that she was not that good, my desires would have an example to follow: I could then get her away from the shelter of her purity, her reputation, her marriage vows, and her thousand other defences, which at the moment are too strong for me to overcome. What do you say, Sir John?

FALSTAFF

Master Brook, I will first make bold with your money; next, give me your hand; and last, as I am a gentleman, you shall, if you will, enjoy Ford's wife.

Master Brook, first I'll take your money; next, I'll shake your hand; and lastly, I promise as I am a gentleman that you shall, if you want to, have Ford's wife.

FORD

O good sir!

Oh good sir!

FALSTAFF

I say you shall.

I tell you you will.

FORD

Want no money, Sir John; you shall want none.

Don't worry about money, Sir John; you shall have all you want.

FALSTAFF

Want no Mistress Ford, Master Brook; you shall want none. I shall be with her, I may tell you, by her own appointment; even as you came in to me, her assistant or go-between parted from me: I say I shall be with her between ten and eleven; for at that time the jealous rascally knave her husband will be forth. Come you to me at night; you shall

Don't worry about Mistress Ford, Master Brook; you will have all of her that you want. I can tell you that I will be visiting her at her own invitation; just as you came in to see me, her assistant or messenger was leaving; I'll tell you I will be with her between ten and eleven; at that time the jealous rascally knave, her husband, will be out. Come to me at night; I'll know how I speed.

FORD
I am blest in your acquaintance. Do you know Ford, sir?

FALSTAFF
Hang him, poor cuckoldly knave! I know him not: yet I wrong him to call him poor; they say the jealous wittolly knave hath masses of money; for the which his wife seems to me well-favored. I will use her as the key of the cuckoldly rogue's coffer; and there's my harvest-home.

FORD
I would you knew Ford, sir, that you might avoid him
if you saw him.

FALSTAFF
Hang him, mechanical salt-butter rogue! I will stare him out of his wits; I will awe him with my cudgel: it shall hang like a meteor o'er the cuckold's horns. Master Brook, thou shalt know I will predominate over the peasant, and thou shalt lie with his wife. Come to me soon at night. Ford's a knave, and I will aggravate his style; thou, Master Brook, shalt know him for knave and cuckold. Come to me soon at night.

Exit

FORD
What a damned Epicurean rascal is this! My heart is ready to crack with impatience. Who says this is improvident jealousy? my wife hath sent to him; the hour is fixed; the match is made. Would any man have thought this? See the hell of having a false woman! My bed shall be abused, my coffers ransacked, my reputation gnawn at; and I shall not only receive this villanous wrong, but stand under the adoption of abominable terms, and by him that does me this wrong. Terms! names! Amaimon sounds well; Lucifer, well; Barbason, well; yet they are devils' additions, the names of fiends: but Cuckold! Wittol!--Cuckold! the devil himself hath not such a name. Page is an ass, a secure ass: he will trust his wife; he will not be jealous. I will

let you know how I get on.

I'm lucky to know you. Do you know Ford, sir?

Damn him, poor cheated on knave! I don't know him: but I shouldn't call him poor; I hear that the jealous blameworthy knave has pots of money; and his wife seems very willing for me to have some. I will use her as the key to get into the cuckolded scoundrel's money chest; that's where I'll reap my harvest.

*I wish you knew Ford, sir, so that you could avoid him
if you saw him.*

Damn him, the vulgar social climbing scoundrel! I will stare the fellow down; I will intimidate him with my club; it will hang like a falling star over his cheated head. Master Brook, I promise you that I will triumph over this peasant, and you shall sleep with his wife. Come to me one night soon. Ford's a knave, and I shall make him worse; you, Master Brook, will see that he is a knave and a cuckold. Come and see me one night soon.

What damned dirty rascal is this? My heart is ready to burst with anger. Nobody can say that this is unreasonable jealousy. My wife has written to him, the time has been fixed, the match has been made. Would any man have imagined this? You see the hell of having a false woman: my bed will be polluted, my money chests ransacked, my reputation ruined, and I shall not only suffer this disgraceful wrong, but be called revolting names, by the one who is doing it to me. Terms! Names! Amaimon sounds good, and Lucifer, and Barbason, but they are all names of the devil. But cuckold! Willing cuckold! The devil himself isn't called such things. Page is a fool, a complacent fool: he will trust his wife, he will not be jealous. I would rather trust a Fleming with my

rather trust a Fleming with my butter, Parson Hugh
the Welshman with my cheese, an Irishman with
my
aqua-vitae bottle, or a thief to walk my ambling
gelding, than my wife with herself; then she plots,
then she ruminates, then she devises; and what they
think in their hearts they may effect, they will
break their hearts but they will effect. God be
praised for my jealousy! Eleven o'clock the hour.
I will prevent this, detect my wife, be revenged on
Falstaff, and laugh at Page. I will about it;
better three hours too soon than a minute too late.
Fie, fie, fie! cuckold! cuckold! cuckold!

Exit

butter, Parson Hugh the
Welshman with my cheese, an Irishman with my
whiskey bottle, or a thief to exercise my walking
horse, than trust my wife with herself. Now she
plots, then she thinks, then she invents; and what
they think in their hearts they will do,
they will break their hearts to achieve. May heaven
be praised for making me jealous! Eleven o'clock is
the time: I will stop this, catch out my wife, have
revenge on
Falstaff, and laugh at Page. I'll get going; better
to be three hours early than one minute too late.
Damn, damn, damn; cheated, cheated, cheated!

SCENE III. A field near Windsor.

Enter DOCTOR CAIUS and RUGBY

DOCTOR CAIUS   PAGE
Jack Rugby!

RUGBY
Sir?

DOCTOR CAIUS
Vat is de clock, Jack?

RUGBY
'Tis past the hour, sir, that Sir Hugh promised to
meet.

DOCTOR CAIUS
By gar, he has save his soul, dat he is no come; he
has pray his Pible well, dat he is no come: by gar,
Jack Rugby, he is dead already, if he be come.

RUGBY
He is wise, sir; he knew your worship would kill
him, if he came.

DOCTOR CAIUS
By gar, de herring is no dead so as I vill kill him.
Take your rapier, Jack; I vill tell you how I vill kill
him.

RUGBY
Alas, sir, I cannot fence.

DOCTOR CAIUS
Villany, take your rapier.

RUGBY
Forbear; here's company.

Enter Host, SHALLOW, SLENDER, and PAGE

Host
Bless thee, bully doctor!

SHALLOW
Save you, Master Doctor Caius!

Jack Rugby!

Sir?

What's the time, Jack?

It is past the time, sir, that Sir Hugh promised he would be here.

By God, he has saved his soul by not coming; he has prayed wisely, by not coming: by God, Jack Rugby, he's a dead man, if he comes here.

He is sensible, sir; he knew your worship would kill him, if he came.

By God, there's no herring as dead as I would kill him. Take your sword, Jack; I'll show you how I will kill him.

Alas, sir, I cannot fence.

You villain, take your sword.

Stop it; we have company.

God bless you, good doctor!

God save you, Master Doctor Caius!

Now, good master doctor!

SLENDER
Give you good morrow, sir.

DOCTOR CAIUS
Vat be all you, one, two, tree, four, come for?

Host
To see thee fight, to see thee foin, to see thee traverse; to see thee here, to see thee there; to see thee pass thy punto, thy stock, thy reverse, thy distance, thy montant. Is he dead, my Ethiopian? is he dead, my Francisco? ha, bully! What says my AEsculapius? my Galen? my heart of elder? ha! is he dead, bully stale? is he dead?

DOCTOR CAIUS
By gar, he is de coward Jack priest of de vorld; he is not show his face.

Host
Thou art a Castalion-King-Urinal. Hector of Greece, my boy!

DOCTOR CAIUS
I pray you, bear vitness that me have stay six or seven, two, tree hours for him, and he is no come.

SHALLOW
He is the wiser man, master doctor: he is a curer of souls, and you a curer of bodies; if you should fight, you go against the hair of your professions. Is it not true, Master Page?

PAGE
Master Shallow, you have yourself been a great fighter, though now a man of peace.

SHALLOW
Bodykins, Master Page, though I now be old and of the peace, if I see a sword out, my finger itches to make one. Though we are justices and doctors and churchmen, Master Page, we have some salt of our youth in us; we are the sons of women, Master Page.

PAGE
'Tis true, Master Shallow.

Now, good master doctor!

Good day to you, sir.

What have you four all come here for?

To see you fight, to see you lunge, to see you dance from side to side and see you here, to see you there; to see you thrust, stick, slash, keep your distance, thrust upwards. Is he dead, my black bearded one? Is he dead, my Frenchman? Ha, good! What do you say, Aesculapius? Galen? My elderflower? Ha! Is he dead, my joke? Is he dead?

By God, he is a cowardly monkey of a priest; he doesn't dare to show his face.

You are a Spanish pisspot. Hector of Greece, my boy!

Please, be my witnesses that I have waited six or seven, two, three hours for him, and he has not come.

He has more sense than you, master doctor: he takes care of souls, and you take care of bodies; if you fight you're both going against your trades. Don't you agree, Master Page?

Master Shallow, you yourself have been a great fighter, though now you are a man of peace.

My goodness, Master Page, although I am now old and peaceful, if I see a drawn sword my fingers itch to join in. Although we are justices and doctors and clergymen, Master Page, we still have a bit of our youthful strength in us; we are still human, Master Page.

That's true, Master Shallow.

SHALLOW

It will be found so, Master Page. Master Doctor Caius, I am come to fetch you home. I am sworn of the peace: you have showed yourself a wise physician, and Sir Hugh hath shown himself a wise and patient churchman. You must go with me, master doctor.

It will be proved, Master Page. Master Doctor Caius, I have come to take you home. I am sworn to keep the peace: you have shown yourself to be a wise physician, and Sir Hugh has shown himself to be a wise and careful clergyman. You must come with me, master doctor.

Host

Pardon, guest-justice. A word, Mounseur Mockwater.

Excuse me, my magistrate guest. A word, Mr Stalepiss.

DOCTOR CAIUS

Mock-vater! vat is dat?

Stalepiss? What does that mean?

Host

Mock-water, in our English tongue, is valour, bully.

Stalepiss, in English, means bravery, old chap.

DOCTOR CAIUS

By gar, den, I have as mush mock-vater as de Englishman. Scurvy jack-dog priest! by gar, me vill cut his ears.

By God, then, I have as much stale piss as the Englishman. Rascally mongrel priest! By God, I shall cut his ears off.

Host

He will clapper-claw thee tightly, bully.

He'll give you a good whopping, old man.

DOCTOR CAIUS

Clapper-de-claw! vat is dat?

Whopping! What is that?

Host

That is, he will make thee amends.

It means that he will apologise to you.

DOCTOR CAIUS

By gar, me do look he shall clapper-de-claw me; for, by gar, me vill have it.

By God, he certainly shall give me a good whopping; I'll insist on it.

Host

And I will provoke him to't, or let him wag.

I'll make him do it, or he'll have to run for it.

DOCTOR CAIUS

Me tank you for dat.

Thank you for that.

Host

And, moreover, bully, [aside]--but first, master guest, and
Master Page, and eke Cavaleiro Slender, go you through the town to Frogmore.

*And, what's more, old chap [aside]–but first, master guest, and
Master Page, and also the gallant Slender, go through the town to Frogmore.*

PAGE

Sir Hugh is there, is he?

That's where Sir Hugh is, is it?

Host
He is there: see what humour he is in; and I will
bring the doctor about by the fields. Will it do well?

*He is: see what sort of mood he is in; and I will
bring the doctor round the long way. Can you play
your part?*

SHALLOW
We will do it.

We will do it.

PAGE SHALLOW SLENDER
Adieu, good master doctor.

Goodbye, good master doctor.

Exeunt PAGE, SHALLOW, and SLENDER

DOCTOR CAIUS
By gar, me vill kill de priest; for he speak for a
jack-an-ape to Anne Page.

*By God, I will kill the priest; he spoke like a
monkey to Anne Page.*

Host
Let him die: sheathe thy impatience, throw cold
water on thy choler: go about the fields with me
through Frogmore: I will bring thee where Mistress
Anne Page is, at a farm-house a-feasting; and thou
shalt woo her. Cried game; said I well?

*Let him die: put away your anger, throw cold
water on your temper: come round the fields with
me to Frogmore: I will lead you to where Mistress
Anne Page is, dining at a farmhouse; and you
will woo her. Are you up for it? Do you like the
idea?*

DOCTOR CAIUS
By gar, me dank you for dat: by gar, I love you;
and I shall procure-a you de good guest, de earl,
de knight, de lords, de gentlemen, my patients.

*By God, I thank you for that: by God, I like you;
I'll get you some good guests, earls,
knights, lords, gentlemen, all my patients.*

Host
For the which I will be thy adversary toward Anne
Page. Said I well?

*And in return I'll ruin your chances with Anne
Page. How does that sound?*

DOCTOR CAIUS
By gar, 'tis good; vell said.

By God, that sounds good; well said.

Host
Let us wag, then.

Let's go then.

DOCTOR CAIUS
Come at my heels, Jack Rugby.

Follow on behind, Jack Rugby.

Exeunt

Act 3

SCENE I. A field near Frogmore.

Enter SIR HUGH EVANS and SIMPLE

SIR HUGH EVANS
I pray you now, good master Slender's serving-man,
and friend Simple by your name, which way have you
looked for Master Caius, that calls himself doctor of
physic?

SIMPLE
Marry, sir, the pittie-ward, the park-ward, every
way; old Windsor way, and every way but the town
way.

SIR HUGH EVANS
I most fehemently desire you you will also look that
way.

SIMPLE
I will, sir.

Exit

SIR HUGH EVANS
'Pless my soul, how full of chollors I am, and
trempling of mind! I shall be glad if he have
deceived me. How melancholies I am! I will knog
his urinals about his knave's costard when I have
good opportunities for the ork. 'Pless my soul!

Sings
To shallow rivers, to whose falls
Melodious birds sings madrigals;
There will we make our peds of roses,
And a thousand fragrant posies.
To shallow--
Mercy on me! I have a great dispositions to cry.

Sings
Melodious birds sing madrigals--
When as I sat in Pabylon--
And a thousand vagram posies.
To shallow & c.

Re-enter SIMPLE

SIMPLE

Now I ask you, good master Slender's servant,
who I understand is called Simple, whereabouts
have you
looked for Master Caius, who calls himself a doctor
of medicine?

Well, sir, in the church district, the park district,
every place; out towards old Windsor, and
everywhere except for the town.

I certainly want you to look there
as well.

I will, sir.

Goodness me, how full of sadness I am, and
my head is spinning: I will be glad if he has
dodged me. How sad I am! I will
wrap his balls around his filthy head when I
get a chance. Bless my soul!

To shallow rivers, by whose falls
sweet birds sing madrigals;
there we will make carpets of roses,
and a thousand fragrant bouquets,
to shallow—
Dear me! I feel as though I'm going to cry—

Sweet birds sing madrigals—
when I sat in Babylon—
and a thousand sweet bouquets,
to shallow, etc.

Yonder he is coming, this way, Sir Hugh.

SIR HUGH EVANS
He's welcome.

Sings
To shallow rivers, to whose falls-
Heaven prosper the right! What weapons is he?

SIMPLE
No weapons, sir. There comes my master, Master
Shallow, and another gentleman, from Frogmore,
over
the stile, this way.

SIR HUGH EVANS
Pray you, give me my gown; or else keep it in your
arms.

Enter PAGE, SHALLOW, and SLENDER

SHALLOW
How now, master Parson! Good morrow, good Sir
Hugh.
Keep a gamester from the dice, and a good student
from his book, and it is wonderful.

SLENDER
[Aside] Ah, sweet Anne Page!

PAGE
'Save you, good Sir Hugh!

SIR HUGH EVANS
'Pless you from his mercy sake, all of you!

SHALLOW
What, the sword and the word! do you study them
both, master parson?

PAGE
And youthful still! in your doublet and hose this
raw rheumatic day?

SIR HUGH EVANS
There is reasons and causes for it.

PAGE
We are come to you to do a good office, master
parson.

He's over there, coming this way, Sir Hugh.

He's welcome.

To shallow rivers, to whose falls–
May God help the righteous! What weapons is he
carrying?

He has no weapons, sir. Here comes my master,
Master
Shallow, and another gentleman, from Frogmore,
over the stile, coming this way.

Please, give me my gown; or hold it in your arms.

Hello there, master Parson! Good day, good Sir
Hugh,
Keep the gambler away from the dice, and a good
student away from his books, and all will be well.

Ah, sweet Anne Page!

God bless you, good Sir Hugh!

May he show you all his mercy!

What, the sword and the word! Are you a student of
both, master parson?

And you're still young! Wearing your shirt and
stockings on this bone chilling day?

I have my reasons for it.

We have come to do you a good turn, master
parson.

SIR HUGH EVANS
Fery well: what is it?

Very good: what is it?

PAGE
Yonder is a most reverend gentleman, who, belike
having received wrong by some person, is at most
odds with his own gravity and patience that ever
you
saw.

*Over there is a very holy gentleman, who, probably
because somebody has treated him badly, is as
out of sorts with his own temper and position as
anyone
you ever saw.*

SHALLOW
I have lived fourscore years and upward; I never
heard a man of his place, gravity and learning, so
wide of his own respect.

*I have lived eighty years and more; I never
heard of a man of his position, seriousness and
learning, who was so different to his usual self.*

SIR HUGH EVANS
What is he?

Who is he?

PAGE
I think you know him; Master Doctor Caius, the
renowned French physician.

*I think you know him; Master Doctor Caius, the
famous French physician.*

SIR HUGH EVANS
Got's will, and his passion of my heart! I had as
lief you would tell me of a mess of porridge.

*By God, and the passion he puts in my heart! I
would care as much if you told me it was a bowl of
porridge.*

PAGE
Why?

Why?

SIR HUGH EVANS
He has no more knowledge in Hibocrates and
Galen,
--and he is a knave besides; a cowardly knave as
you
would desires to be acquainted withal.

*He has no knowledge of medical texts,
besides he is a scoundrel; as cowardly a knave
as you could wish to meet.*

PAGE
I warrant you, he's the man should fight with him.

I'm telling you, he's the man you're going to fight.

SHALLOW
[Aside] O sweet Anne Page!

Oh sweet Anne Page!

SHALLOW
It appears so by his weapons. Keep them asunder:
here comes Doctor Caius.

*It would seem so from his weapons. Keep them
apart: here comes Doctor Caius.*

Enter Host, DOCTOR CAIUS, and RUGBY

PAGE
Nay, good master parson, keep in your weapon.

No, good master parson, keep your sword in its

SHALLOW
So do you, good master doctor.

Host
Disarm them, and let them question: let them keep
their limbs whole and hack our English.

DOCTOR CAIUS
I pray you, let-a me speak a word with your ear.
Vherefore vill you not meet-a me?

SIR HUGH EVANS
[Aside to DOCTOR CAIUS] Pray you, use your
patience:
[Aloud] in good time.

DOCTOR CAIUS
By gar, you are de coward, de Jack dog, John ape.

SIR HUGH EVANS
[Aside to DOCTOR CAIUS] Pray you let us not be
laughing-stocks to other men's humours; I desire
you
in friendship, and I will one way or other make you
amends.

Aloud
I will knog your urinals about your knave's
cockscomb
for missing your meetings and appointments.

DOCTOR CAIUS
Diable! Jack Rugby,--mine host de Jarteer,--have I
not stay for him to kill him? have I not, at de place
I did appoint?

SIR HUGH EVANS
As I am a Christians soul now, look you, this is the
place appointed: I'll be judgement by mine host of
the Garter.

Host
Peace, I say, Gallia and Gaul, French and Welsh,
soul-curer and body-curer!

DOCTOR CAIUS
Ay, dat is very good; excellent.

Host

sheath.

You do the same, good master doctor.

*Disarm them, and let them argue: let them keep
their limbs whole and just hack our language about.*

*Please, let me have a word in your ear.
Why will you not fight me?*

Please, remain calm. [Aloud] All in good time

*By God, you are a coward, a useless dog, a dirty
monkey.*

*Please don't let's be
at the mercy of other men's moods; I want to be
friends, and I'll find a way of making it up to you.*

*I will smash your balls around your knave's head
for not keeping your appointments.*

*You devil! Jack Rugby—my host of the Garter—
haven't I been waiting here to kill him? Haven't I, at
the place I named?*

*As I am a Christian soul, look you, this is
the place chosen: I'll stand by the judgement of my
host of the Garter.*

*Peace, I ask, Gallia and Gaul, French and Welsh,
parson and doctor!*

Ah, that's very good; excellent.

Peace, I say! hear mine host of the Garter. Am I politic? am I subtle? am I a Machiavel? Shall I lose my doctor? no; he gives me the potions and the motions. Shall I lose my parson, my priest, my Sir Hugh? no; he gives me the proverbs and the no-verbs. Give me thy hand, terrestrial; so. Give me thy hand, celestial; so. Boys of art, I have deceived you both; I have directed you to wrong places: your hearts are mighty, your skins are whole, and let burnt sack be the issue. Come, lay their swords to pawn. Follow me, lads of peace; follow, follow, follow.

SHALLOW
Trust me, a mad host. Follow, gentlemen, follow.

SLENDER
[Aside] O sweet Anne Page!

Exeunt SHALLOW, SLENDER, PAGE, and Host

DOCTOR CAIUS
Ha, do I perceive dat? have you make-a de sot of us, ha, ha?

SIR HUGH EVANS
This is well; he has made us his vlouting-stog. I desire you that we may be friends; and let us knog our prains together to be revenge on this same scall, scurvy cogging companion, the host of the Garter.

DOCTOR CAIUS
By gar, with all my heart. He promise to bring me where is Anne Page; by gar, he deceive me too.

SIR HUGH EVANS
Well, I will smite his noddles. Pray you, follow.

Exeunt

Peace, I say! Listen to the landlord of the Garter. Am I a politician? Am I cunning? Am I a Machiavelli? Shall I lose my doctor? No, he gives me medicine and purgatives. Shall I lose my parson, my priest, my Sir Hugh? No, he gives me the proverbs and tells me what not to do. Give me your hand, earthly man; give me your hand, man of heaven. You clever boys, I have deceived you both: I sent you to the wrong places; you have shown you have great hearts, your skins are undamaged, and let a good drink be the result. Come on, put aside your swords. Come with me, peaceful lads; follow, follow, follow.

Believe me, this is a mad landlord. Follow him, gentlemen, follow him.

Oh sweet Anne Page!

Ha, do I read this correctly? Have you made fools out of us, hey, hey?

Well, that's what he's done; he is made us a laughingstock. I would like us to be friends; and let us rack our brains together to get revenge on this scabby, filthy, deceiving villain, the landlord of the Garter.

By God, with all my heart. He promised to bring me to Anne Page: by God, he deceived me too.

Well, I shall bash his head in. Please, come with me.

SCENE II. A street.

Enter MISTRESS PAGE and ROBIN

MISTRESS PAGE
Nay, keep your way, little gallant; you were wont to
be a follower, but now you are a leader. Whether
had you rather lead mine eyes, or eye your master's
heels?

ROBIN
I had rather, forsooth, go before you like a man
than follow him like a dwarf.

MISTRESS PAGE
O, you are a flattering boy: now I see you'll be a
courtier.

Enter FORD

FORD
Well met, Mistress Page. Whither go you?

MISTRESS PAGE
Truly, sir, to see your wife. Is she at home?

FORD
Ay; and as idle as she may hang together, for want
of company. I think, if your husbands were dead,
you two would marry.

MISTRESS PAGE
Be sure of that,--two other husbands.

FORD
Where had you this pretty weather-cock?

MISTRESS PAGE
I cannot tell what the dickens his name is my
husband had him of. What do you call your knight's
name, sirrah?

ROBIN
Sir John Falstaff.

FORD
Sir John Falstaff!

MISTRESS PAGE

No, keep going, my little soldier; you used to be a follower, but now you are a leader. Would you rather lead my eyes, or have your eyes on your master's heels?

I would rather, I swear, go ahead of you like a man than behind him like a dwarf.

Oh, you are a silver tongued boy: I can see you will make a courtier.

Hello there, Mistress Page. Where are you going?

To tell you the truth, sir, to see your wife. Is she at home?

Yes, and as idle as she can be without dying, for lack of company. I think, if your husbands were dead, you two would be married.

You can be sure of that–to two other husbands.

Where did you get this pretty little ornament?

I can't remember what the hell the name is of the fellow my husband had him from. What was your knight's name, sir?

Sir John Falstaff.

Sir John Falstaff!

He, he; I can never hit on's name. There is such a
league between my good man and he! Is your wife at
home indeed?

FORD
Indeed she is.

MISTRESS PAGE
By your leave, sir: I am sick till I see her.

Exeunt MISTRESS PAGE and ROBIN

FORD
Has Page any brains? hath he any eyes? hath he any
thinking? Sure, they sleep; he hath no use of them.
Why, this boy will carry a letter twenty mile, as
easy as a cannon will shoot point-blank twelve
score. He pieces out his wife's inclination; he
gives her folly motion and advantage: and now she's
going to my wife, and Falstaff's boy with her. A
man may hear this shower sing in the wind. And
Falstaff's boy with her! Good plots, they are laid;
and our revolted wives share damnation together.
Well; I will take him, then torture my wife, pluck
the borrowed veil of modesty from the so seeming
Mistress Page, divulge Page himself for a secure and
wilful Actaeon; and to these violent proceedings all
my neighbours shall cry aim.

Clock heard
The clock gives me my cue, and my assurance bids me
search: there I shall find Falstaff: I shall be
rather praised for this than mocked; for it is as
positive as the earth is firm that Falstaff is
there: I will go.

Enter PAGE, SHALLOW, SLENDER, Host, SIR HUGH EVANS, DOCTOR CAIUS, and RUGBY

SHALLOW PAGE & C
Well met, Master Ford.

FORD
[aside] Trust me, a good knot: [aloud] I have good
cheer at home;
and I pray you all go with me.

SHALLOW

---

*That's the one; I can never remember the name. My husband
and he are thick as thieves! So, your wife is
definitely at home?*

She certainly is.

Then excuse me, sir: I am desperate to see her.

*Hasn't Page.any brains? Hasn't he any eyes? Can't
he think? I'm certain they're all asleep: he has no
use for them. Why, this boy could carry a letter
twenty miles as easily as you could hit a barn door
with a cannon. He is actually helping his wife's plan
along; he is giving her weakness motive and
opportunity: and now she's going to my wife, and
taking Falstaff's boy with her. A man
can hear the storm coming. And Falstaff's boy with
her! These are good plots! They are prepared; and
our cheating wives will be dammed together. Well, I
will show him, then torment my wife, pull the
borrowed veil of modesty from the innocent looking
Mistress Page, show up Page himself as an
overconfident and blameworthy cuckold; and in all
these rowdy events my neighbours will praise my
efforts.*

*[Clock strikes]
The clock says that it is time, and my certainty tells
me to look: I shall find Falstaff there. I would
rather be applauded for this than mocked, for I am
on very solid ground thinking Falstaff is there. I will
go.*

Hello there, Master Ford.

*[aside] Well, here's a pretty mob: [aloud] I've
plenty to eat and drink at home;
please, why don't you all come with me.*

I must excuse myself, Master Ford.

SLENDER
And so must I, sir: we have appointed to dine with
Mistress Anne, and I would not break with her for
more money than I'll speak of.

SHALLOW
We have lingered about a match between Anne
Page and
my cousin Slender, and this day we shall have our
answer.

SLENDER
I hope I have your good will, father Page.

PAGE
You have, Master Slender; I stand wholly for you:
but my wife, master doctor, is for you altogether.

DOCTOR CAIUS
Ay, be-gar; and de maid is love-a me: my nursh-a
Quickly tell me so mush.

Host
What say you to young Master Fenton? he capers,
he
dances, he has eyes of youth, he writes verses, he
speaks holiday, he smells April and May: he will
carry't, he will carry't; 'tis in his buttons; he
will carry't.

PAGE
Not by my consent, I promise you. The gentleman
is
of no having: he kept company with the wild prince
and Poins; he is of too high a region; he knows too
much. No, he shall not knit a knot in his fortunes
with the finger of my substance: if he take her,
let him take her simply; the wealth I have waits on
my consent, and my consent goes not that way.

FORD
I beseech you heartily, some of you go home with
me
to dinner: besides your cheer, you shall have
sport; I will show you a monster. Master doctor,
you shall go; so shall you, Master Page; and you,
Sir Hugh.

You must excuse me, Master Ford.

*And me, sir: we have a date to dine with
Mistress Anne, and I wouldn't break it off for
the world.*

*We have been hoping for a match between Anne
Page and
my cousin Slender, and today we'll know the
answer.*

I hope I have your support, father Page.

*You have, Master Slender; I'm completely on your
side:
but my wife, master doctor, is completely on yours.*

*Yes, by God; and the girl loves me: Mistress
Quickly told me as much.*

*What would you say to young Master Fenton? He
can leap,
he can dance, he has a young man's eyes, he writes
verses, he speaks in a jolly way, he has the
freshness of spring: he'll win, he'll win; you can see
it in his face; he will win.*

*Not with my agreement, I can assure you. The
gentleman is
no catch: he used to hang out with the wild Prince
of Wales and Poins; he moves in too high circles;
he is too experienced. No, he will not patch up his
fortunes with my material: if he wants her
he can have her on her own; my wealth depends on
my decision, and I don't decide that way.*

*I really must insist that some of you come home with
me
for dinner: besides the food and drink, you shall be
entertained; I'll show you a freak. Master doctor,
you shall come; so shall you, Master Page; and
you, Sir Hugh.*

SHALLOW
Well, fare you well: we shall have the freer wooing at Master Page's.

Exeunt SHALLOW, and SLENDER

DOCTOR CAIUS
Go home, John Rugby; I come anon.

Exit RUGBY

Host
Farewell, my hearts: I will to my honest knight Falstaff, and drink canary with him.

Exit

FORD
[Aside] I think I shall drink in pipe wine first with him; I'll make him dance. Will you go, gentles?

All
Have with you to see this monster.

Exeunt

*Well, have a good time: this will give us more freedom
to woo at Master Page's place.*

Go home, John Rugby; I'll come in a while.

Goodbye, dear boys: I'm going to my good knight Falstaff, to drink sherry with him.

*I think I shall have a little tipple with him;
I'll make him dance. Are you coming, gentlemen?*

We'll come with you to see this freak.

SCENE III. A room in FORD'S house.

Enter MISTRESS FORD and MISTRESS PAGE

                                             Enter ROBIN

MISTRESS FORD
What, John! What, Robert!

MISTRESS PAGE
Quickly, quickly! is the buck-basket--

MISTRESS FORD
I warrant. What, Robin, I say!

Enter Servants with a basket

MISTRESS PAGE
Come, come, come.

MISTRESS FORD
Here, set it down.

MISTRESS PAGE
Give your men the charge; we must be brief.

MISTRESS FORD
Marry, as I told you before, John and Robert, be
ready here hard by in the brew-house: and when I
suddenly call you, come forth, and without any
pause
or staggering take this basket on your shoulders:
that done, trudge with it in all haste, and carry
it among the whitsters in Datchet-mead, and there
empty it in the muddy ditch close by the Thames
side.

MISTRESS PAGE
You will do it?

MISTRESS FORD
I ha' told them over and over; they lack no
direction. Be gone, and come when you are called.

Exeunt Servants

MISTRESS PAGE
Here comes little Robin.

Hello, John! Hello, Robert!

Quickly, quickly! Is the laundry basket–

I'm sure of it. Hello, Robin, where are you!

Come on, hurry up.

Here, put it down.

Give your men your orders; we must hurry.

Now, as I told you before, John and Robert, be ready close by in the outhouse; and when I suddenly call you, come out and without pausing or hesitating take this basket on your shoulders. When you've done that, walk off with it quickly, and carry it to the bleachers in Datchet Meadow, and there tip the contents into the muddy ditch by the side of the Thames.

You'll do it?

I've told them over and over again; they don't need any more orders. Go, and come when you are called.

Here comes little Robin.

MISTRESS FORD

How now, my eyas-musket! what news with you?

Hello, my baby hunting hawk! What's the news?

ROBIN

My master, Sir John, is come in at your back-door,
Mistress Ford, and requests your company.

*My master, Sir John, has come in by the back door,
Mistress Ford, and wants to see you.*

MISTRESS PAGE

You little Jack-a-Lent, have you been true to us?

You little imp, have you stayed loyal to us?

ROBIN

Ay, I'll be sworn. My master knows not of your
being here and hath threatened to put me into
everlasting liberty if I tell you of it; for he
swears he'll turn me away.

*Yes, I'll swear it. My master doesn't know that
you're here and has threatened to sack me
permanently if I tell you he is; he swears
he'll lay me off.*

MISTRESS PAGE

Thou'rt a good boy: this secrecy of thine shall be
a tailor to thee and shall make thee a new doublet
and hose. I'll go hide me.

*You're a good boy: your discretion will be
a tailor for you and get you a new jacket
and stockings. I'll go and hide.*

MISTRESS FORD

Do so. Go tell thy master I am alone.

Do that. Go and tell your master I'm alone.

Exit ROBIN

Mistress Page, remember you your cue.

Mistress Page, don't forget your cue.

MISTRESS PAGE

I warrant thee; if I do not act it, hiss me.

I promise I won't; if I miss it, boo me.

Exit

MISTRESS FORD

Go to, then: we'll use this unwholesome humidity,
this gross watery pumpion; we'll teach him to know
turtles from jays.

*Off you go then: we'll trick this unhealthy sweatbag,
this gross watery pumpkin; we'll teach him the
difference between tarts and respectable women.*

Enter FALSTAFF

FALSTAFF

Have I caught thee, my heavenly jewel? Why, now
let
me die, for I have lived long enough: this is the
period of my ambition: O this blessed hour!

*Have I got you, my heavenly jewel? Why, now
I can die, for I have lived long enough: this is the
pinnacle of my dreams: oh what a happy time!*

MISTRESS FORD

O sweet Sir John!

Oh sweet Sir John!

FALSTAFF

Mistress Ford, I cannot cog, I cannot prate,
Mistress Ford. Now shall I sin in my wish: I would
thy husband were dead: I'll speak it before the
best lord; I would make thee my lady.

MISTRESS FORD
I your lady, Sir John! alas, I should be a pitiful lady!

FALSTAFF
Let the court of France show me such another. I see
how thine eye would emulate the diamond: thou
hast
the right arched beauty of the brow that becomes
the
ship-tire, the tire-valiant, or any tire of
Venetian admittance.

MISTRESS FORD
A plain kerchief, Sir John: my brows become
nothing
else; nor that well neither.

FALSTAFF
By the Lord, thou art a traitor to say so: thou
wouldst make an absolute courtier; and the firm
fixture of thy foot would give an excellent motion
to thy gait in a semi-circled farthingale. I see
what thou wert, if Fortune thy foe were not, Nature
thy friend. Come, thou canst not hide it.

MISTRESS FORD
Believe me, there is no such thing in me.

FALSTAFF
What made me love thee? let that persuade thee
there's something extraordinary in thee. Come, I
cannot cog and say thou art this and that, like a
many of these lisping hawthorn-buds, that come like
women in men's apparel, and smell like
Bucklersbury
in simple time; I cannot: but I love thee; none
but thee; and thou deservest it.

MISTRESS FORD
Do not betray me, sir. I fear you love Mistress Page.

FALSTAFF
Thou mightst as well say I love to walk by the
Counter-gate, which is as hateful to me as the reek
of a lime-kiln.

---

*Mistress Ford, I cannot lie, I don't have a silver
tongue, Mistress Ford. Now I shall be a sinner by
wishing: I wish your husband was dead: I'll say it in
front of the highest in the land; I want you to be my
lady.*

*Me your lady, Sir John! I'm afraid I would be a very
poor lady!*

*Let the French court show me one as good. I can
see
that your eyes are like diamonds: you have
the perfect curves to your brow that would suit
the most elaborate headdresses of the Venetian
fashion.*

*A plain headscarf, Sir John: nothing else suits my
brow;
and that doesn't look particularly good.*

*By God, it's treason to say so: you
would make a perfect courtier: and your
perfect posture would make you look very good
as you walked in a fashionable dress. I can see
what you should have been, if fortune had been as
kind to you
as nature has been. Come on, you can't hide it.*

Believe me, I have no such qualities.

*What made me fall in love with you? That should
show you there's something wonderful in you.
Come, I cannot lie and say you are this and that,
like so many of these mincing poets, who are like
women dressed as men, and smell like a perfume
shop
in summertime; I cannot: but I love you; nobody
but you; and you are worthy of my love.*

*Don't lie to me, sir. I'm afraid you love Mistress
Page.*

*You might as well say that I like to walk past
the debtors' prison, which smells as bad to me as
the stench of a lime kiln.*

MISTRESS FORD
Well, heaven knows how I love you; and you shall one
day find it.

Well, God knows how much I love you; and one day you shall know it too.

FALSTAFF
Keep in that mind; I'll deserve it.

Remember that; I'll earn it.

MISTRESS FORD
Nay, I must tell you, so you do; or else I could not be in that mind.

No, I must tell you, so you do; otherwise I couldn't think that way.

ROBIN
[Within] Mistress Ford, Mistress Ford! here's Mistress Page at the door, sweating and blowing and
looking wildly, and would needs speak with you presently.

Mistress Ford, Mistress Ford! Here is Mistress Page at the door, sweating and puffing and staring madly, and she says she must speak to you at once.

FALSTAFF
She shall not see me: I will ensconce me behind the arras.

She can't see me: I will hide behind the curtain.

MISTRESS FORD
Pray you, do so: she's a very tattling woman.

Please, do: she's a terrible gossip.

FALSTAFF hides himself

Re-enter MISTRESS PAGE and ROBIN

What's the matter? how now!

What's all this? What's going on!

MISTRESS PAGE
O Mistress Ford, what have you done? You're shamed,
you're overthrown, you're undone for ever!

Oh Mistress Ford, what have you done? You're shamed, you're ruined, you're lost forever!

MISTRESS FORD
What's the matter, good Mistress Page?

Whatever is the matter, good Mistress Page?

MISTRESS PAGE
O well-a-day, Mistress Ford! having an honest man to your husband, to give him such cause of suspicion!

Oh what a terrible thing, Mistress Ford! With a good man as your husband, you give him such grounds for suspicion!

MISTRESS FORD
What cause of suspicion?

What grounds have I given him?

MISTRESS PAGE
What cause of suspicion! Out pon you! how am I

What grounds have you given him! Don't play the

mistook in you!

MISTRESS FORD
Why, alas, what's the matter?

MISTRESS PAGE
Your husband's coming hither, woman, with all the officers in Windsor, to search for a gentleman that he says is here now in the house by your consent, to take an ill advantage of his assence: you are undone.

MISTRESS FORD
'Tis not so, I hope.

MISTRESS PAGE
Pray heaven it be not so, that you have such a man here! but 'tis most certain your husband's coming, with half Windsor at his heels, to search for such a one. I come before to tell you. If you know yourself clear, why, I am glad of it; but if you have a friend here convey, convey him out. Be not amazed; call all your senses to you; defend your reputation, or bid farewell to your good life for ever.

MISTRESS FORD
What shall I do? There is a gentleman my dear friend; and I fear not mine own shame so much as his
peril: I had rather than a thousand pound he were out of the house.

MISTRESS PAGE
For shame! never stand 'you had rather' and 'you had rather:' your husband's here at hand, bethink you of some conveyance: in the house you cannot hide him. O, how have you deceived me! Look, here
is a basket: if he be of any reasonable stature, he may creep in here; and throw foul linen upon him, as
if it were going to bucking: or--it is whiting-time --send him by your two men to Datchet-mead.

MISTRESS FORD
He's too big to go in there. What shall I do?

FALSTAFF
[Coming forward] Let me see't, let me see't, O, let me see't! I'll in, I'll in. Follow your friend's

---

innocent: how mistaken I was about you!

Why, whatever can the matter be?

Your husband is coming here, woman, with all the officers of Windsor, to look for a gentleman that he says is in the house now with your permission in order to get up to no good while he's gone: you are lost.

I hope not.

Please God it may not be true, that you have a man here as they say! But it's certainly true that your husband is coming, with half of Windsor following him, to look for such a man. I ran ahead to tell you. If you know that you are innocent, why, I'm very glad; but if you have a friend here you had better get him out. Don't be panicked; get your wits about you; defend your reputation, or say goodbye to your pleasant life for ever.

What shall I do? There is a man here, my dear friend; and I'm not so worried about my own shame as
the danger for him: I would give a thousand pounds for him to be out of the house.

For heaven's sake! Don't waste time saying 'I wish this' and 'I wish that.' Your husband is right here, think of some way to get him away: you can't hide him in the house. Oh how you have misled me! Look, here
is a basket: if he's any reasonable size, he can creep in here; throw the dirty linen on top of him as if it was going to the wash; or–it is the time of year for bleaching–
send him with your two men to Datchet Meadow.

He's too big to get in there. What shall I do?

Let me see it, let me see it quick, let me see it! I'll get in, I'll get in. Do as your friend counsel. I'll in.

says, I'll get in.

MISTRESS PAGE
What, Sir John Falstaff! Are these your letters,
knight?

*What, Sir John Falstaff! Are these your letters,
knight?*

FALSTAFF
I love thee. Help me away. Let me creep in here.
I'll never--

*I love you, help me escape. Let me get in here.
I'll never--*

Gets into the basket; they cover him with foul linen

MISTRESS PAGE
Help to cover your master, boy. Call your men,
Mistress Ford. You dissembling knight!

*Helped cover up your master, boy. Call your men,
Mistress Ford. You cheating knight!*

MISTRESS FORD
What, John! Robert! John!

Hello, John! Robert! John!

Exit ROBIN

Re-enter Servants

Go take up these clothes here quickly. Where's the
cowl-staff? look, how you drumble! Carry them to
the laundress in Datchet-mead; quickly, come.

*Go and take away these clothes, quickly. Where's
the carrying pole? Look how you dawdle! Take
them to the laundress in Datchet Meadow; quickly,
get going.*

Enter FORD, PAGE, DOCTOR CAIUS, and SIR HUGH EVANS

FORD
Pray you, come near: if I suspect without cause,
why then make sport at me; then let me be your jest;
I deserve it. How now! whither bear you this?

*You stick close to me: if my suspicions are
groundless, then you can make fun of me; let me be
the bottom of your jokes; I would deserve it. What's
this! Where are you taking this?*

Servant
To the laundress, forsooth.

To the laundress, of course.

MISTRESS FORD
Why, what have you to do whither they bear it?
You
were best meddle with buck-washing.

*What's it got to do with you where they're taking it?
You should be thinking about washing bucks.*

FORD
Buck! I would I could wash myself of the buck!
Buck, buck, buck! Ay, buck; I warrant you, buck;
and of the season too, it shall appear.

*Bucks! I wish I could wash away the buck!
Buck, buck, buck! Yes, buck; I should think it is a
buck; it's the season for it as I'll show.*

Exeunt Servants with the basket
Gentlemen, I have dreamed to-night; I'll tell you my

Gentlemen, I had a dream last night; I'll tell you my

dream. Here, here, here be my keys: ascend my
chambers; search, seek, find out: I'll warrant
we'll unkennel the fox. Let me stop this way first.

Locking the door

So, now uncape.

PAGE
Good Master Ford, be contented: you wrong
yourself too much.

FORD
True, Master Page. Up, gentlemen: you shall see
sport anon: follow me, gentlemen.

Exit

SIR HUGH EVANS
This is fery fantastical humours and jealousies.

DOCTOR CAIUS
By gar, 'tis no the fashion of France; it is not
jealous in France.

PAGE
Nay, follow him, gentlemen; see the issue of his
search.

Exeunt PAGE, DOCTOR CAIUS, and SIR HUGH EVANS

MISTRESS PAGE
Is there not a double excellency in this?

MISTRESS FORD
I know not which pleases me better, that my
husband
is deceived, or Sir John.

MISTRESS PAGE
What a taking was he in when your husband asked
who
was in the basket!

MISTRESS FORD
I am half afraid he will have need of washing; so
throwing him into the water will do him a benefit.

MISTRESS PAGE
Hang him, dishonest rascal! I would all of the same

---

*dream. Here, here, here are my keys: go up to my
bedrooms, search, seek, discover: I swear
we'll unearth the fox. Let me block up this escape
first.*

So, now let's uncover him.

*Good Master Ford, calm down: you are getting in a
state.*

*That's true, Master Page. Up you go, gentlemen:
you'll see the quarry soon: follow me, gentlemen.*

These are amazing moods and jealousies.

*By God, we are not like this in France; we are not
jealous in France.*

*Come on and follow him, gentlemen; let's see the
results of his search.*

Isn't this doubly good?

*I don't know which pleases me more, that my
husband
has been tricked, or that Sir John has.*

*Imagine what he must have felt when your husband
asked what
was in the basket!*

*My only regret is that he will need a wash; so
throwing him into the water will do him good.*

Hang him, the dishonest rascal! I wish everyone

strain were in the same distress.

like him was in the same boat.

MISTRESS FORD
I think my husband hath some special suspicion of Falstaff's being here; for I never saw him so gross in his jealousy till now.

I think my husband had some special reason to think that Falstaff was here; I never saw him so openly jealous before.

MISTRESS PAGE
I will lay a plot to try that; and we will yet have more tricks with Falstaff: his dissolute disease will scarce obey this medicine.

I'll play a trick to find that out; and we'll have some more fun with Falstaff: he's so awful that this alone won't be enough to teach him.

MISTRESS FORD
Shall we send that foolish carrion, Mistress Quickly, to him, and excuse his throwing into the water; and give him another hope, to betray him to another punishment?

Shall we send that silly bitch, Mistress Quickly, to him, apologise for his being thrown into the water, and hold out more hope, to trap him into another punishment?

MISTRESS PAGE
We will do it: let him be sent for to-morrow, eight o'clock, to have amends.

Let's do it: let's send for him tomorrow at eight o'clock, to apologise.

Re-enter FORD, PAGE, DOCTOR CAIUS, and SIR HUGH EVANS

FORD
I cannot find him: may be the knave bragged of that he could not compass.

I can't find him: maybe the scoundrel was boasting of things that he couldn't manage.

MISTRESS PAGE
[Aside to MISTRESS FORD] Heard you that?

Did you hear that?

MISTRESS FORD
You use me well, Master Ford, do you?

This is a good way to treat me, is it Master Ford?

FORD
Ay, I do so.

Yes, it is.

MISTRESS FORD
Heaven make you better than your thoughts!

May heaven make you better than your thoughts!

FORD
Amen!

Amen!

MISTRESS PAGE
You do yourself mighty wrong, Master Ford.

You have done yourself a great wrong, Master Ford.

FORD
Ay, ay; I must bear it.

Yes, yes; I must put up with it.

SIR HUGH EVANS

If there be any pody in the house, and in the chambers, and in the coffers, and in the presses, heaven forgive my sins at the day of judgment!

If there is anybody in the house, in the bedrooms, in the chests, in the drawers, then may heaven forgive my sins on Judgement Day!

DOCTOR CAIUS
By gar, nor I too: there is no bodies.

By God, mine neither: there's nobody here.

PAGE
Fie, fie, Master Ford! are you not ashamed? What spirit, what devil suggests this imagination? I would not ha' your distemper in this kind for the wealth of Windsor Castle.

Come now, Master Ford! Aren't you ashamed? What spirit, what devil stirred up your imagination? I wouldn't want to have your sort of feelings for all the treasure in Windsor Castle.

FORD
'Tis my fault, Master Page: I suffer for it.

I'm in the wrong, Master Page: I suffer for it.

SIR HUGH EVANS
You suffer for a pad conscience: your wife is as honest a 'omans as I will desires among five thousand, and five hundred too.

You're suffering from a bad conscience: your wife is as honest a woman as one could hope to find amongst five thousand, or even five hundred.

DOCTOR CAIUS
By gar, I see 'tis an honest woman.

By God, I can see she's an honest woman.

FORD
Well, I promised you a dinner. Come, come, walk in
the Park: I pray you, pardon me; I will hereafter make known to you why I have done this. Come, wife; come, Mistress Page. I pray you, pardon me; pray heartily, pardon me.

*Well, I promised you a dinner. Come on, we'll walk in
the Park until it's ready: please forgive me; I will tell you later why I have done this. Come, wife; come, Mistress Page. Please, forgive me; I'm begging you, forgive me.*

PAGE
Let's go in, gentlemen; but, trust me, we'll mock him. I do invite you to-morrow morning to my house
to breakfast: after, we'll a-birding together; I have a fine hawk for the bush. Shall it be so?

*Let's go in, gentlemen; but, believe me, we'll make fun of him. I'd like to invite you to come to my house for breakfast
tomorrow morning; afterwards, we'll go hunting together; I have a good hawk for flushing out game.*

FORD
Any thing.

Whatever you like.

SIR HUGH EVANS
If there is one, I shall make two in the company.

If anyone is going, I will be a second member of the party.

DOCTOR CAIUS
If dere be one or two, I shall make-a the turd.

If there are going to be one or two, I shall be the third.

FORD
Pray you, go, Master Page.

Come on, Master Page.

SIR HUGH EVANS
I pray you now, remembrance tomorrow on the lousy
knave, mine host.

*Now don't forget, tomorrow we will take revenge on that
lousy scoundrel, the landlord.*

DOCTOR CAIUS
Dat is good; by gar, with all my heart!

That's good; by God, definitely!

SIR HUGH EVANS
A lousy knave, to have his gibes and his mockeries!

A lousy scoundrel, with his sneers and jokes!

Exeunt

SCENE IV. A room in PAGE'S house.

Enter FENTON and ANNE PAGE

FENTON
I see I cannot get thy father's love;
Therefore no more turn me to him, sweet Nan.

I see I'll never get your father's approval;
so don't ask me to approach him again, sweet Anne.

ANNE PAGE
Alas, how then?

Alas, what shall we do then?

FENTON
Why, thou must be thyself.
He doth object I am too great of birth--,
And that, my state being gall'd with my expense,
I seek to heal it only by his wealth:
Besides these, other bars he lays before me,
My riots past, my wild societies;
And tells me 'tis a thing impossible
I should love thee but as a property.

Well, you must decide for yourself.
His objection is that I am too high born,
and that as my estate is loaded with debt
I am trying to improve it with his wealth:
besides that, he has other objections to me,
my former riotous behaviour and my wild company;
he tells me that he'll never believe
that I love you for anything but your money.

ANNE PAGE
May be he tells you true.

Perhaps he's right.

FENTON
No, heaven so speed me in my time to come!
Albeit I will confess thy father's wealth
Was the first motive that I woo'd thee, Anne:
Yet, wooing thee, I found thee of more value
Than stamps in gold or sums in sealed bags;
And 'tis the very riches of thyself
That now I aim at.

He's not, may heaven strike me dead if he is!
I must admit that your father's wealth
was what inspired me to woo you, Anne:
but in the process I found you are worth more
than golden coins or moneybags;
it is the riches of your personality
which I want now.

ANNE PAGE
Gentle Master Fenton,
Yet seek my father's love; still seek it, sir:
If opportunity and humblest suit
Cannot attain it, why, then,--hark you hither!

Gentle Master Fenton,
carry on trying for my father's approval:
if the circumstances and humble pleading
cannot get it, why then--listen to me!

They converse apart

Enter SHALLOW, SLENDER, and MISTRESS QUICKLY

SHALLOW   **SLENDER**
Break their talk, Mistress Quickly: my kinsman
shall
speak for himself.

Break up their conversation, Mistress Quickly: my relative
will speak for himself.

I'll make a shaft or a bolt on't: 'slid, 'tis but venturing.

I'll have a stab at it, I'll succeed one way or the other.

FALLOW
Be not dismayed.

Don't despair.

SLENDER
No, she shall not dismay me: I care not for that, but that I am afeard.

No, she can't make me despair: the only thing that can set me back is my own fear.

MISTRESS QUICKLY
Hark ye; Master Slender would speak a word with you.

Listen; Master Slender would like to speak to you.

ANNE PAGE
I come to him.

I'm coming.

Aside
This is my father's choice.
O, what a world of vile ill-favor'd faults
Looks handsome in three hundred pounds a-year!

*This is the one my father wants for me.
Oh, how many revolting ugly flaws
can be covered up by three hundred pounds a year!*

MISTRESS QUICKLY
And how does good Master Fenton? Pray you, a word with you.

And how is good Master Fenton? Please, I want a word with you.

SHALLOW
She's coming; to her, coz. O boy, thou hadst a father!

She's coming; go to her, cousin. Oh boy, you had a father!

SLENDER
I had a father, Mistress Anne; my uncle can tell you good jests of him. Pray you, uncle, tell Mistress Anne the jest, how my father stole two geese out of a pen, good uncle.

I had a father, Mistress Anne; my uncle can tell you some good stories about it. Please, uncle, tell Mistress Anne the story of how my father stole two geese out of a pen, good uncle.

SHALLOW
Mistress Anne, my cousin loves you.

Mistress Anne, my cousin loves you.

SLENDER
Ay, that I do; as well as I love any woman in Gloucestershire.

Yes I do; as much as I love any woman in Gloucestershire.

SHALLOW
He will maintain you like a gentlewoman.

He will keep you like a gentlewoman.

SLENDER
Ay, that I will, come cut and long-tail, under the degree of a squire.

Yes I will, come what may, as befits the title of a squire.

SHALLOW
He will make you a hundred and fifty pounds jointure.

He will set up a legacy of one hundred and fifty pounds for you.

ANNE PAGE
Good Master Shallow, let him woo for himself.

Good Master Shallow, let him do his own wooing.

SHALLOW
Marry, I thank you for it; I thank you for that good comfort. She calls you, coz: I'll leave you.

Thank you for saying that; thank you for those kind words. She is asking for you, cousin: I'll leave you.

ANNE PAGE
Now, Master Slender,--

Now, Master Slender–

SLENDER
Now, good Mistress Anne,--

Now, good Mistress Anne–

ANNE PAGE
What is your will?

What is your will?

SLENDER
My will! 'od's heartlings, that's a pretty jest indeed! I ne'er made my will yet, I thank heaven; I am not such a sickly creature, I give heaven praise.

My will! By God, that's a nice joke! I have never made a will, thank heavens; thank heavens, I am not ill.

ANNE PAGE
I mean, Master Slender, what would you with me?

I mean, Master Slender, what are your intentions towards me?

SLENDER
Truly, for mine own part, I would little or nothing with you. Your father and my uncle hath made motions: if it be my luck, so; if not, happy man be his dole! They can tell you how things go better than I can: you may ask your father; here he comes.

Truly, for my part, I have no intentions towards you. Your father and my uncle have set this up; if I have the luck to get you, good; if not, good luck to the one who does! They can tell you better than I how matters progress: you can ask your father; here he comes.

Enter PAGE and MISTRESS PAGE

PAGE
Now, Master Slender: love him, daughter Anne. Why, how now! what does Master Fenton here? You wrong me, sir, thus still to haunt my house: I told you, sir, my daughter is disposed of.

Now, Master Slender: love him, daughter Anne. Why, what's this! What is Master Fenton doing here? You're doing wrong, sir, to still hang around my house: I told you, sir, my daughter is spoken for.

FENTON
Nay, Master Page, be not impatient.

No, Master Page, don't be so hasty.

MISTRESS PAGE
Good Master Fenton, come not to my child.

Good Master Fenton, don't make advances to my child.

PAGE

She is no match for you.

You shan't marry her.

FENTON
Sir, will you hear me?

Sir, will you listen to me?

PAGE
No, good Master Fenton.
Come, Master Shallow; come, son Slender, in.
Knowing my mind, you wrong me, Master Fenton.

No, good Master Fenton.
Come, Master Shallow; come, son Slender, let's go in. You know my intentions, and so you are insulting me, Master Fenton.

Exeunt PAGE, SHALLOW, and SLENDER

MISTRESS QUICKLY
Speak to Mistress Page.

Speak to Mistress Page.

FENTON
Good Mistress Page, for that I love your daughter
In such a righteous fashion as I do,
Perforce, against all cheques, rebukes and manners,
I must advance the colours of my love
And not retire: let me have your good will.

Good Mistress Page, as I love your daughter so completely,
I must carry on pressing my suit in the face of all censure, rebukes and conventions, and I cannot retreat: give me your blessing.

ANNE PAGE
Good mother, do not marry me to yond fool.

Good mother, do not marry me to that fool over there.

MISTRESS PAGE
I mean it not; I seek you a better husband.

I don't intend to; I'm looking for a better husband for you.

MISTRESS QUICKLY
That's my master, master doctor.

She means my master, the master doctor.

ANNE PAGE
Alas, I had rather be set quick i' the earth
And bowl'd to death with turnips!

Oh no, I would rather be buried up to the neck in the ground and stoned to death with turnips!

MISTRESS PAGE
Come, trouble not yourself. Good Master Fenton,
I will not be your friend nor enemy:
My daughter will I question how she loves you,
And as I find her, so am I affected.
Till then farewell, sir: she must needs go in;
Her father will be angry.

Now now, don't trouble yourself. Good Master Fenton, I will be neither your friend nor your enemy: I will question my daughter about her love for you, and I will act accordingly.
Until then farewell, sir: she must go inside; her father will be angry.

FENTON
Farewell, gentle mistress: farewell, Nan.

Farewell, gentle mistress: farewell, Nan.

Exeunt MISTRESS PAGE and ANNE PAGE

MISTRESS QUICKLY
This is my doing, now: 'Nay,' said I, 'will you cast

I sorted this out: 'No,' I said, 'will you throw

away your child on a fool, and a physician? Look on
Master Fenton:' this is my doing.

FENTON
I thank thee; and I pray thee, once to-night
Give my sweet Nan this ring: there's for thy pains.

MISTRESS QUICKLY
Now heaven send thee good fortune!

Exit FENTON
A kind heart he hath: a woman would run through
fire and water for such a kind heart. But yet I
would my master had Mistress Anne; or I would
Master Slender had her; or, in sooth, I would Master
Fenton had her; I will do what I can for them all
three; for so I have promised, and I'll be as good
as my word; but speciously for Master Fenton.
Well,
I must of another errand to Sir John Falstaff from
my two mistresses: what a beast am I to slack it!

Exit

your daughter away on a fool and a doctor?
Look at Master Fenton.' This is my doing.

Thank you; and please, at some point tonight
give my sweet Nan this ring: take this for your
trouble.

May Heaven bless you with good luck!

He has a kind heart: a woman will run through
Fire and water for such a kind heart. And yet I
would like my master to have Mistress Anne; or
for Master Slender to have; or, in fact, for Master
Fenton to have her; I will do what I can for all three
of them; that's what I've promised, and I'll be as
good as my word; but I'll work especially hard for
Master Fenton. Well, I must run another errand to
Sir John Falstaff from my two mistresses: what a
slowcoach I am to have left it until now!

SCENE V. A room in the Garter Inn.

Enter FALSTAFF and BARDOLPH

FALSTAFF
Bardolph, I say,--

BARDOLPH
Here, sir.

FALSTAFF
Go fetch me a quart of sack; put a toast in't.

Exit BARDOLPH

Have I lived to be carried in a basket, like a
barrow of butcher's offal, and to be thrown in the
Thames? Well, if I be served such another trick,
I'll have my brains ta'en out and buttered, and give
them to a dog for a new-year's gift. The rogues
slighted me into the river with as little remorse as
they would have drowned a blind bitch's puppies,
fifteen i' the litter: and you may know by my size
that I have a kind of alacrity in sinking; if the
bottom were as deep as hell, I should down. I had
been drowned, but that the shore was shelvy and
shallow,--a death that I abhor; for the water swells
a man; and what a thing should I have been when I
had been swelled! I should have been a mountain of
mummy.

Re-enter BARDOLPH with sack

BARDOLPH
Here's Mistress Quickly, sir, to speak with you.

FALSTAFF
Let me pour in some sack to the Thames water; for
my
belly's as cold as if I had swallowed snowballs for
pills to cool the reins. Call her in.

BARDOLPH
Come in, woman!

Enter MISTRESS QUICKLY

MISTRESS QUICKLY
By your leave; I cry you mercy: give your worship

Bardolph, I want–

I'm here, sir.

Go and get me a quart of sherry; put some toast in it.

Has it come to this, for me to be carried in a basket like a barrowful of butcher's offal, and to be thrown in the Thames? Well, if I ever fall for trick like that again, I'll have my brains taken out and buttered, and give then to a dog as a New Year's present. The scoundrels chucked me into the river caring as little as if they were drowning the puppies of a blind bitch, with fifteen in the litter; and you can see from my size that I'm rather good at sinking: if the bottom went as far down as hell, I would reach it. I would have been drowned except down the shore shelved and was shallow– I would hate to die like that: drowned men swell up; and what should I look like swollen up! I would look like a mountain of meat.

Here's Mistress Quickly, sir, to speak with you.

Let me add some sherry to the Thames water; my belly is as cold as if I had swallowed snowballs as pills to cool my kidneys. Tell her to come in.

Come in, woman!

With your permission; I thank you for it: good day

good morrow.

to your worship.

FALSTAFF
Take away these chalices. Go brew me a pottle of
sack finely.

*Take away these thimble sized cups. Go and brew
me a good two quarts of sack.*

BARDOLPH
With eggs, sir?

With eggs, sir?

FALSTAFF
Simple of itself; I'll no pullet-sperm in my brewage.

*I'll take it straight; I don't want chicken sperm in my
drink.*

Exit BARDOLPH

How now!

Now then!

MISTRESS QUICKLY
Marry, sir, I come to your worship from Mistress
Ford.

*Well, sir, I have come to your worship from
Mistress Ford.*

FALSTAFF
Mistress Ford! I have had ford enough; I was
thrown
into the ford; I have my belly full of ford.

*Mistress Ford! I have had enough of fords; I was
thrown
into the ford; my belly is full of ford.*

MISTRESS QUICKLY
Alas the day! good heart, that was not her fault:
she does so take on with her men; they mistook
their erection.

*A bad business! Dear man, that was not her fault:
she is furious with her men; they misunderstood
their instructions.*

FALSTAFF
So did I mine, to build upon a foolish woman's
promise.

So did I, setting store by a foolish woman's promise.

MISTRESS QUICKLY
Well, she laments, sir, for it, that it would yearn
your heart to see it. Her husband goes this morning
a-birding; she desires you once more to come to her
between eight and nine: I must carry her word
quickly: she'll make you amends, I warrant you.

*Well, she is very sorry for it, sir, it would break
your heart to see it. Her husband is going out
hunting this morning; she wants you to come to her
again between eight and nine: I must take her your
answer
quickly: she'll make it up to you, I promise you.*

FALSTAFF
Well, I will visit her: tell her so; and bid her
think what a man is: let her consider his frailty,
and then judge of my merit.

*Well, I will visit: tell her I will; and tell her
to think how frail men can be,
and to judge my merits in that context.*

MISTRESS QUICKLY
I will tell her.

I will tell her.

FALSTAFF

Do so. Between nine and ten, sayest thou?

Do so. Between nine and ten, did you say?

MISTRESS QUICKLY
Eight and nine, sir.

Eight and nine, sir.

FALSTAFF
Well, be gone: I will not miss her.

Well, on your way: I'll be there.

MISTRESS QUICKLY
Peace be with you, sir.

Peace be with you, sir.

Exit

FALSTAFF
I marvel I hear not of Master Brook; he sent me word
to stay within: I like his money well. O, here he comes.

I'm surprised I haven't heard from Master Brook; he sent me a message
to wait for him: I'm keen on his money. Oh, here he comes.

Enter FORD

FORD
Bless you, sir!

Bless you, sir!

FALSTAFF
Now, Master Brook, you come to know what hath passed
between me and Ford's wife?

Now, Master Brook, have you heard of what happened between
myself and Ford's wife?

FORD
That, indeed, Sir John, is my business.

Indeed Sir John, that is why I have come.

FALSTAFF
Master Brook, I will not lie to you: I was at her house the hour she appointed me.

Master Brook, I will not lie to you: I was at her house at the time she instructed.

FORD
And sped you, sir?

And did you get on well, sir?

FALSTAFF
Very ill-favoredly, Master Brook.

Very badly, Master Brook.

FORD
How so, sir? Did she change her determination?

Why was that, sir? Did she change her mind?

FALSTAFF
No, Master Brook; but the peaking Cornuto her husband, Master Brook, dwelling in a continual 'larum of jealousy, comes me in the instant of our encounter, after we had embraced, kissed, protested,

No, Master Brook; but that slinking cuckold, her husband, Master Brook, who lives in a continuous jealous fear, came to me just as things were coming to the boil, after we had hugged, kissed, spoken our

and, as it were, spoke the prologue of our comedy; and at his heels a rabble of his companions, thither provoked and instigated by his distemper, and, forsooth, to search his house for his wife's love.

FORD
What, while you were there?

FALSTAFF
While I was there.

FORD
And did he search for you, and could not find you?

FALSTAFF
You shall hear. As good luck would have it, comes in one Mistress Page; gives intelligence of Ford's approach; and, in her invention and Ford's wife's distraction, they conveyed me into a buck-basket.

FORD
A buck-basket!

FALSTAFF
By the Lord, a buck-basket! rammed me in with foul
shirts and smocks, socks, foul stockings, greasy napkins; that, Master Brook, there was the rankest compound of villanous smell that ever offended nostril.

FORD
And how long lay you there?

FALSTAFF
Nay, you shall hear, Master Brook, what I have suffered to bring this woman to evil for your good. Being thus crammed in the basket, a couple of Ford's
knaves, his hinds, were called forth by their mistress to carry me in the name of foul clothes to Datchet-lane: they took me on their shoulders; met the jealous knave their master in the door, who asked them once or twice what they had in their basket: I quaked for fear, lest the lunatic knave would have searched it; but fate, ordaining he should be a cuckold, held his hand. Well: on went he
for a search, and away went I for foul clothes. But mark the sequel, Master Brook: I suffered the pangs

feelings, and, as it were, gone through the prologue of the comedy; he had with him a mob of friends, who were ordered and egged on by his temper to search his house for his wife's lover.

What, while you were there?

While I was there.

And he searched for you, and could not find you?

I'll tell you. As good luck had it, in came one Mistress Page; she gave warning of Ford's coming; and with her cunning and Ford's wife's panic, they put me into a laundry basket.

A laundry basket!

By God, a laundry basket! They shoved me in with dirty
shirts and smocks, socks, foul stockings, greasy napkins; Master Brook, together they made the most disgusting
mixture of smells that ever revolted anyone's nose.

And how long were you in there?

You shall hear, Master Brook, what I have endured to turn this woman bad, for your good. As I was squashed in this basket, a couple of Ford's scoundrels, his servants, were ordered by their
mistress to take me, disguised as dirty clothes, to Datchet Lane; they lifted me on their shoulders; they met that jealous knave their master in the doorway, who asked them a couple of times what was in the basket. I was shaking with fear that the mad knave would search it; but fate, deciding that he should be betrayed, held back. Well, he carried on with his search, and I went off disguised as dirty clothes. But note what happened afterwards, Master Brook: I had to put up with the

of three several deaths; first, an intolerable
fright, to be detected with a jealous rotten
bell-wether; next, to be compassed, like a good
bilbo, in the circumference of a peck, hilt to
point, heel to head; and then, to be stopped in,
like a strong distillation, with stinking clothes
that fretted in their own grease: think of that,--a
man of my kidney,--think of that,--that am as
subject
to heat as butter; a man of continual dissolution
and thaw: it was a miracle to scape suffocation.
And in the height of this bath, when I was more
than
half stewed in grease, like a Dutch dish, to be
thrown into the Thames, and cooled, glowing hot,
in that surge, like a horse-shoe; think of
that,--hissing hot,--think of that, Master Brook.

FORD
In good sadness, I am sorry that for my sake you
have sufferd all this. My suit then is desperate;
you'll undertake her no more?

FALSTAFF
Master Brook, I will be thrown into Etna, as I have
been into Thames, ere I will leave her thus. Her
husband is this morning gone a-birding: I have
received from her another embassy of meeting;
'twixt
eight and nine is the hour, Master Brook.

FORD
'Tis past eight already, sir.

FALSTAFF
Is it? I will then address me to my appointment.
Come to me at your convenient leisure, and you
shall
know how I speed; and the conclusion shall be
crowned with your enjoying her. Adieu. You shall
have her, Master Brook; Master Brook, you shall
cuckold Ford.

Exit

FORD
Hum! ha! is this a vision? is this a dream? do I
sleep? Master Ford awake! awake, Master Ford!
there's a hole made in your best coat, Master Ford.
This 'tis to be married! this 'tis to have linen

---

*fear of three separate deaths. Firstly
there was the terrible fright that I would be
discovered by that jealous
diseased ass; next, I was bent double
like a good sword forced into a jar, hilt to point,
head to heels; I was forced in with stinking clothes
like something being boiled in their own grease–
think of that–
a man of my type–think of that–who is as affected by
heat as butter; a man who is always boiling and
sweating.
it was a miracle I didn't suffocate. And
at the worst of this boiling, when I was more than
half stewed in grease, like a Dutch dish, I was
thrown into the Thames and cooled, glowing hot,
into the river, like a horseshoe–think of that–
hissing hot–think of that, Master Brook!*

*I am genuinely sorry that you have suffered
all this for my sake. That's the end of my wooing
then; you won't try her again?*

*Master Brook, I will be thrown into a volcano, as I
have been into the Thames, before I will give up like
this. Her
husband has gone hunting this morning: I have
been summoned to another date by her; between
eight and nine is the time, Master Brook.*

It's gone eight already, sir.

*Is it? Then I will go and keep my appointment.
Come to me when you can, and I will tell you
how I got on; and the outcome of it all will be
that you shall have her. Goodbye. You shall
have her, Master Brook; Master Brook, you shall
cheat on Ford.*

*Hum! Ha! Is this an hallucination? Is this a dream?
Am I asleep? Master Ford wake up! Wake up,
Master Ford! There is a fault in your perfect life,
Master Ford. This is what marriage is like! This is*

and buck-baskets! Well, I will proclaim myself
what I am: I will now take the lecher; he is at my
house; he cannot 'scape me; 'tis impossible he
should; he cannot creep into a halfpenny purse,
nor into a pepper-box: but, lest the devil that
guides him should aid him, I will search
impossible places. Though what I am I cannot
avoid,
yet to be what I would not shall not make me tame:
if I have horns to make one mad, let the proverb go
with me: I'll be horn-mad.

Exit

*what it's like to have linen
and laundry baskets! Well, I will reveal myself for
who I am: I will now have the lecher; he is at my
house; he can't escape me; is impossible for him
to do; he can't creep into a change purse,
nor into a pepperpot: but, unless the devil that
guides him helps him, I will search
every possible place. Though I can't help what I am,
I'll be dammed if I become what I am not:
if being cheated on makes one mad, let me be
the proof of it: I shall go mad.*

Act 4

SCENE I. A street.

Enter MISTRESS PAGE, MISTRESS QUICKLY, and WILLIAM PAGE

MISTRESS PAGE
Is he at Master Ford's already, think'st thou?

MISTRESS QUICKLY
Sure he is by this, or will be presently: but,
truly, he is very courageous mad about his throwing
into the water. Mistress Ford desires you to come
suddenly.

MISTRESS PAGE
I'll be with her by and by; I'll but bring my young
man here to school. Look, where his master comes;
'tis a playing-day, I see.

Enter SIR HUGH EVANS
How now, Sir Hugh! no school to-day?

SIR HUGH EVANS
No; Master Slender is let the boys leave to play.

MISTRESS QUICKLY
Blessing of his heart!

MISTRESS PAGE
Sir Hugh, my husband says my son profits nothing
in
the world at his book. I pray you, ask him some
questions in his accidence.

SIR HUGH EVANS
Come hither, William; hold up your head; come.

MISTRESS PAGE
Come on, sirrah; hold up your head; answer your
master, be not afraid.

SIR HUGH EVANS
William, how many numbers is in nouns?

WILLIAM PAGE
Two.

MISTRESS QUICKLY
Truly, I thought there had been one number more,
because they say, "Od's nouns.'

Do you think he's already at Master Ford's?

He surely is by now, or will be very shortly: but, truly, he's boiling mad about being thrown into the water. Mistress Ford wants you to come at once.

I'll be with her soon; first I have to take my young man here to school. Look, here comes his teacher; it's a holiday, I see.

Hello there, Sir Hugh! No school today?

No; Master Slender has given the boys the day off.

Bless his heart!

Sir Hugh, my husband says that my son is learning nothing from his books. Please, test him on his pronunciation.

Come here, William: hold your head up: come on.

Come on, lad; hold your head up; answer your teacher, don't be shy.

William, how many types of nouns are there?

Two.

Well, I thought there was one more than that, because they say, "odd nouns."

SIR HUGH EVANS
Peace your tattlings! What is 'fair,' William?

Stop your chatter! How do you say 'fair,' William?

WILLIAM PAGE
Pulcher.

Pulcher.

MISTRESS QUICKLY
Polecats! there are fairer things than polecats, sure.

Polecats! There are certainly fairer things than that.

SIR HUGH EVANS
You are a very simplicity 'oman: I pray you peace. What is 'lapis,' William?

You are a very backward woman: please be quiet. What is 'lapis,' William?

WILLIAM PAGE
A stone.

A stone.

SIR HUGH EVANS
And what is 'a stone,' William?

And what is 'a stone,' William?

WILLIAM PAGE
A pebble.

A pebble.

SIR HUGH EVANS
No, it is 'lapis:' I pray you, remember in your prain.

No, it is 'lapis:' please, keep that in mind.

WILLIAM PAGE
Lapis.

Lapis.

SIR HUGH EVANS
That is a good William. What is he, William, that does lend articles?

Well done William. What's the one, William, that lends articles?

WILLIAM PAGE
Articles are borrowed of the pronoun, and be thus declined, Singulariter, nominativo, hic, haec, hoc.

Articles are borrowed from the pronoun, and are declined like this: singular, nominative, hic, haec, hoc.

SIR HUGH EVANS
Nominativo, hig, hag, hog; pray you, mark: genitivo, hujus. Well, what is your accusative case?

*Nominative, hig, hag, hog; make sure you remember.
genitive, humus. Well, what is the accusative case?*

WILLIAM PAGE
Accusativo, hinc.

Accusative, hind.

SIR HUGH EVANS
I pray you, have your remembrance, child, accusative, hung, hang, hog.

Please make sure you remember correctly, child, accusative is hung, hang, hog.

MISTRESS QUICKLY
'Hang-hog' is Latin for bacon, I warrant you.

'Hang–hog' is Latin for bacon, I'll be bound.

SIR HUGH EVANS
Leave your prabbles, 'oman. What is the focative case, William?

Stop your gibbering, woman. What is the vocative case, William?

WILLIAM PAGE
O,--vocativo, O.

Oh, vocative, oh.

SIR HUGH EVANS
Remember, William; focative is caret.

Remember, William; vocative is caret.

MISTRESS QUICKLY
And that's a good root.

And that's a good vegetable.

SIR HUGH EVANS
'Oman, forbear.

Give over, woman.

MISTRESS PAGE
Peace!

Quiet!

SIR HUGH EVANS
What is your genitive case plural, William?

What is the genitive case plural, William?

WILLIAM PAGE
Genitive case!

Genitive case!

SIR HUGH EVANS
Ay.

Yes.

WILLIAM PAGE
Genitive,--horum, harum, horum.

Genitive: horum, harum, horum.

MISTRESS QUICKLY
Vengeance of Jenny's case! fie on her! never name her, child, if she be a whore.

The vengeance of Jenny's case! Down with her! Don't name her, child, if she is a whore.

SIR HUGH EVANS
For shame, 'oman.

For heaven's sake, woman.

MISTRESS QUICKLY
You do ill to teach the child such words: he teaches him to hick and to hack, which they'll do fast enough of themselves, and to call 'horum:' fie upon you!

You shouldn't be teaching the child such words: he teaches him to hick and to hack, which they'll learn quickly enough for themselves, and to call for 'horum', shame on you!

SIR HUGH EVANS
'Oman, art thou lunatics? hast thou no understandings for thy cases and the numbers of the genders? Thou art as foolish Christian creatures as I would desires.

Woman, are you a lunatic? Don't you understand cases, and the numbers of the genders? You are as foolish a Christian as one could wish for.

MISTRESS PAGE
Prithee, hold thy peace.

Please, be quiet.

SIR HUGH EVANS
Show me now, William, some declensions of your pronouns.

Now William, decline some pronouns for me.

WILLIAM PAGE
Forsooth, I have forgot.

I'm afraid I've forgotten.

SIR HUGH EVANS
It is qui, quae, quod: if you forget your 'quies,' your 'quaes,' and your 'quods,' you must be preeches. Go your ways, and play; go.

It is qui, quae, quod: if you forget your 'quies,' your 'quaes,' and your 'quods,' you must be whipped. Off you go and play; go.

MISTRESS PAGE
He is a better scholar than I thought he was.

He's a better student than I thought he was.

SIR HUGH EVANS
He is a good sprag memory. Farewell, Mistress Page.

He has a good lively memory. Goodbye, Mistress Page.

MISTRESS PAGE
Adieu, good Sir Hugh.

Goodbye, good Sir Hugh.

Exit SIR HUGH EVANS

Get you home, boy. Come, we stay too long.

Get back home, boy. Come on, we've been away too long.

Exeunt

SCENE II. A room in FORD'S house.

Enter FALSTAFF and MISTRESS FORD

Why?

FALSTAFF
Mistress Ford, your sorrow hath eaten up my
sufferance. I see you are obsequious in your love,
and I profess requital to a hair's breadth; not
only, Mistress Ford, in the simple
office of love, but in all the accoutrement,
complement and ceremony of it. But are you
sure of your husband now?

MISTRESS FORD
He's a-birding, sweet Sir John.

MISTRESS PAGE
[Within] What, ho, gossip Ford! what, ho!

MISTRESS FORD
Step into the chamber, Sir John.

Exit FALSTAFF

Enter MISTRESS PAGE

MISTRESS PAGE
How now, sweetheart! who's at home besides
yourself?

MISTRESS FORD
Why, none but mine own people.

MISTRESS PAGE
Indeed!

MISTRESS FORD
No, certainly.

Aside to her

Speak louder.

MISTRESS PAGE
Truly, I am so glad you have nobody here.

MISTRESS FORD

*Mistress Ford, your regrets have softened my
suffering.
I see that your love is anxious to please,
and I offer back just the same; not
only, Mistress Ford, in the basic form
of love, but in all its trappings. But are you
sure we're safe from your husband?*

He's bird hunting, sweet Sir John.

Hello there, my old friend Ford! Hello there!

Step into the bedroom, Sir John.

*How's it going, sweetheart! Who's home apart from
you?*

Why, nobody but the servants.

Really!

Yes, really.

Speak louder.

I must say, I am so glad you are alone.

Why?

MISTRESS PAGE
Why, woman, your husband is in his old lunes
again:
he so takes on yonder with my husband; so rails
against all married mankind; so curses all Eve's
daughters, of what complexion soever; and so
buffets
himself on the forehead, crying, 'Peer out, peer
out!' that any madness I ever yet beheld seemed but
tameness, civility and patience, to this his
distemper he is in now: I am glad the fat knight is
not here.

*Why, woman, your husband has his old madness
back:
he is so angry with my husband over there; he rants
against all marriage; he curses all women
of all types; and he bashes himself
on the forehead, shouting, 'show yourself, show
yourself!' in such a way that any other madness I've
seen
seemed just tame calm manners, compared to this
madness he has now: I'm glad the fat knight is not
here.*

MISTRESS FORD
Why, does he talk of him?

Why, is he talking about him?

MISTRESS PAGE
Of none but him; and swears he was carried out, the
last time he searched for him, in a basket; protests
to my husband he is now here, and hath drawn him
and
the rest of their company from their sport, to make
another experiment of his suspicion: but I am glad
the knight is not here; now he shall see his own
foolery.

*Him and no other; he swears that he was carried
out, the
last time he searched for him, in a basket; he insists
to my husband that he is here now, and has taken
him and
the rest of their group away from their hunting, to
put his suspicions to the test again: but I'm glad
the knight is not here; now he'll see how stupid he
is.*

MISTRESS FORD
How near is he, Mistress Page?

How close is he, Mistress Page.

MISTRESS PAGE
Hard by; at street end; he will be here anon.

*Very near; at the end of the street; he'll be here in a
moment.*

MISTRESS FORD
I am undone! The knight is here.

I am lost! The knight is here.

MISTRESS PAGE
Why then you are utterly shamed, and he's but a
dead
man. What a woman are you!--Away with him,
away
with him! better shame than murder.

*Well then you are completely shamed, and he's as
good as
dead. What a woman you are! Get him out, get
him out! Better that there should be shame rather
than murder.*

FORD
Which way should he go? how should I bestow
him?
Shall I put him into the basket again?

*Which way should he go? What shall I do with him?
Shall I put him into the basket again?*

Re-enter FALSTAFF

FALSTAFF

No, I'll come no more i' the basket. May I not go
out ere he come?

MISTRESS PAGE
Alas, three of Master Ford's brothers watch the door
with pistols, that none shall issue out; otherwise
you might slip away ere he came. But what make
you here?

FALSTAFF
What shall I do? I'll creep up into the chimney.

MISTRESS FORD
There they always use to discharge their
birding-pieces. Creep into the kiln-hole.

FALSTAFF
Where is it?

MISTRESS FORD
He will seek there, on my word. Neither press,
coffer, chest, trunk, well, vault, but he hath an
abstract for the remembrance of such places, and
goes to them by his note: there is no hiding you in
the house.

FALSTAFF
I'll go out then.

MISTRESS PAGE
If you go out in your own semblance, you die, Sir
John. Unless you go out disguised--

MISTRESS FORD
How might we disguise him?

MISTRESS PAGE
Alas the day, I know not! There is no woman's
gown
big enough for him otherwise he might put on a hat,
a muffler and a kerchief, and so escape.

FALSTAFF
Good hearts, devise something: any extremity rather
than a mischief.

MISTRESS FORD
My maid's aunt, the fat woman of Brentford, has a
gown above.

*No, I won't go in the basket again. Can't I go
before he gets here?*

*Alas, three of Master Ford's brothers are watching
the door with pistols, so nobody can get out;
otherwise you could have slipped away before he
came. But what are you doing here?*

What shall I do? I'll hide up the chimney.

*They always fire their bird guns
up there. Creep into the oven.*

Where is it?

*He'll look there, I'm sure. Whether you hide in the
cupboard,
strongbox, chest, trunk, well or cellar, he has a
list to help him remember all these places, and
he goes to them in turn: we can't hide you in the
house.*

Then I'll leave.

*If you go out with your usual appearance, you will
die, Sir John. Unless you go out disguised–*

How can we disguise him?

*Alas, I can't think! There is no dress
big enough for him, otherwise he could put on a hat,
a scarf and a bandanna, and so escape.*

*Dear women, think of something: I'll do anything to
avoid being wounded.*

*My maid's aunt, the fat woman of Brentford, has a
dress upstairs.*

MISTRESS PAGE
On my word, it will serve him; she's as big as he
is: and there's her thrummed hat and her muffler
too. Run up, Sir John.

*I swear, that will do him; she's as big as he
is: there's her fringed hat and her scarf
too. Run up there, Sir John.*

MISTRESS FORD
Go, go, sweet Sir John: Mistress Page and I will
look some linen for your head.

*Go, go, sweet Sir John: Mistress Page and I will
find some covering for your head.*

MISTRESS PAGE
Quick, quick! we'll come dress you straight: put
on the gown the while.

*Hurry! We'll come and dress you in a moment: in
the meantime put on the dress.*

Exit FALSTAFF

MISTRESS FORD
I would my husband would meet him in this shape:
he
cannot abide the old woman of Brentford; he swears
she's a witch; forbade her my house and hath
threatened to beat her.

*I hope my husband meets him in this disguise: he
hates the old woman of Brentford; he's convinced
she's a witch; he's banned her from the house and
has
threatened to beat her.*

MISTRESS PAGE
Heaven guide him to thy husband's cudgel, and the
devil guide his cudgel afterwards!

*May heaven lead him to your husband's stick, and
may the devil control the stick after that!*

MISTRESS FORD
But is my husband coming?

But is my husband coming?

MISTRESS PAGE
Ah, in good sadness, is he; and talks of the basket
too, howsoever he hath had intelligence.

*Yes, in all seriousness, he is; he is talking about the
basket
too, however he found out about that.*

MISTRESS FORD
We'll try that; for I'll appoint my men to carry the
basket again, to meet him at the door with it, as
they did last time.

*We'll put that to the test; I'll tell my men to carry the
basket again, and meet him at the door with it, like
they did last time.*

MISTRESS PAGE
Nay, but he'll be here presently: let's go dress him
like the witch of Brentford.

*Well, he'll be here shortly: let's go and dress him
like the witch of Brentford.*

MISTRESS FORD
I'll first direct my men what they shall do with the
basket. Go up; I'll bring linen for him straight.

*First I'll tell my men what they should do with the
basket. Go upstairs; I'll bring linen for him in a
moment.*

Exit

MISTRESS PAGE
Hang him, dishonest varlet! we cannot misuse him

Hang him, the dishonest scoundrel! We can't treat

enough.
We'll leave a proof, by that which we will do,
Wives may be merry, and yet honest too:
We do not act that often jest and laugh;
'Tis old, but true, Still swine eat all the draff.

him badly enough.
What we do will prove
that wives can be merry and still honest:
we don't often play tricks and laugh;
the old proverb is true, the quietest pig gets the
most food.

Exit

Re-enter MISTRESS FORD with two Servants

MISTRESS FORD
Go, sirs, take the basket again on your shoulders:
your master is hard at door; if he bid you set it
down, obey him: quickly, dispatch.

Gentlemen, lift the basket onto your shoulders
again: your master is almost at the door; if he tells
you to put it down, do as he asks: quickly, get going.

Exit

First Servant
Come, come, take it up.

Come on, pick it up.

Second Servant
Pray heaven it be not full of knight again.

Please God let it not to be full of knight again.

First Servant
I hope not; I had as lief bear so much lead.

I hope not; I would just as soon carry lead.

Enter FORD, PAGE, SHALLOW, DOCTOR CAIUS, and SIR HUGH EVANS

FORD
Ay, but if it prove true, Master Page, have you any
way then to unfool me again? Set down the basket,
villain! Somebody call my wife. Youth in a basket!
O you panderly rascals! there's a knot, a ging, a
pack, a conspiracy against me: now shall the devil
be shamed. What, wife, I say! Come, come forth!
Behold what honest clothes you send forth to
bleaching!

Yes, but if I'm right, Master Page, will you still
call me a fool then? Put down the basket,
you rascal! Somebody call my wife. The lover thinks
he's won! Oh you pimping rascals! There's a gang,
a pack, a mob, a conspiracy against me: now the
truth will out. Where are you, wife! Come out, come
out! Let's see the simple clothes you send out to be
bleached!

PAGE
Why, this passes, Master Ford; you are not to go
loose any longer; you must be pinioned.

Why, this is too much, Master Ford; you should not
be allowed out; you must be tied down.

SIR HUGH EVANS
Why, this is lunatics! this is mad as a mad dog!

Why, this is lunacy! He's as mad as a mad dog!

SHALLOW
Indeed, Master Ford, this is not well, indeed.

Indeed, Master Ford, this is not good, not good.

FORD
So say I too, sir.

That's what I say as well, sir.

Re-enter MISTRESS FORD

Come hither, Mistress Ford; Mistress Ford the honest
woman, the modest wife, the virtuous creature, that hath the jealous fool to her husband! I suspect without cause, mistress, do I?

*Come here, Mistress Ford; Mistress Ford the honest
woman, the modest wife, the virtuous creature, who has a jealous fool as a husband! My suspicions are groundless, are they, mistress?*

MISTRESS FORD
Heaven be my witness you do, if you suspect me in any dishonesty.

As heaven is my witness they are, if you suspect me of any dishonesty.

FORD
Well said, brazen-face! hold it out. Come forth, sirrah!

Well said, brass neck! Keep it up. Come out, sir!

Pulling clothes out of the basket

PAGE
This passes!

This beats everything!

MISTRESS FORD
Are you not ashamed? let the clothes alone.

Aren't you ashamed? Leave the clothes alone.

FORD
I shall find you anon.

I'll find you soon.

SIR HUGH EVANS
'Tis unreasonable! Will you take up your wife's clothes? Come away.

This is ridiculous! Will you throw around your wife's clothes? Come away.

FORD
Empty the basket, I say!

I'm telling you, empty the basket!

MISTRESS FORD
Why, man, why?

Why, man, why?

FORD
Master Page, as I am a man, there was one conveyed
out of my house yesterday in this basket: why may not he be there again? In my house I am sure he is: my intelligence is true; my jealousy is reasonable. Pluck me out all the linen.

*Master Page, as sure as I'm standing here, someone was carried
out of my house yesterday in this basket: why shouldn't he be in there again? I am positive he is in my house: my information is true; my jealousy is justified. Take out all the linen.*

MISTRESS FORD
If you find a man there, he shall die a flea's death.

If you find a man in there, he'll be small enough to be crushed like a flea.

PAGE
Here's no man.

There is no man here.

SHALLOW
By my fidelity, this is not well, Master Ford; this wrongs you.

I swear, this is bad, Master Ford; this puts you in the wrong.

SIR HUGH EVANS
Master Ford, you must pray, and not follow the imaginations of your own heart: this is jealousies.

Master Ford, you must pray, and not be led by your own suspicions: this is jealousy.

FORD
Well, he's not here I seek for.

Well, the one I'm looking for isn't here.

PAGE
No, nor nowhere else but in your brain.

No and he's nowhere else except in your brain.

FORD
Help to search my house this one time. If I find not what I seek, show no colour for my extremity; let
me for ever be your table-sport; let them say of me, 'As jealous as Ford, Chat searched a hollow walnut for his wife's leman.' Satisfy me once more; once more search with me.

*Help me search my house this one time. If I don't find what I'm looking for, never defend my madness; let
me forever be a joke; let them say of me, 'Chat searched in a hollow walnut for his wife's lover, as jealous as Ford.' Indulge me one more time; make one more search with me.*

MISTRESS FORD
What, ho, Mistress Page! come you and the old woman
down; my husband will come into the chamber.

*Hello there, Mistress Page! You and the old woman must
come down; my husband wants to come into the bedroom.*

FORD
Old woman! what old woman's that?

Old woman! What old woman is that?

MISTRESS FORD
Nay, it is my maid's aunt of Brentford.

Just my maid's aunt from Brentford.

FORD
A witch, a quean, an old cozening quean! Have I not
forbid her my house? She comes of errands, does she? We are simple men; we do not know what's brought to pass under the profession of fortune-telling. She works by charms, by spells, by the figure, and such daubery as this is, beyond our element we know nothing. Come down, you witch,
you hag, you; come down, I say!

*A witch, a harlot, a cheating old harlot! Haven't I banned her from my house? She comes on errands, does
she? We are simple men; we don't know what goes on under the disguise of
fortune-telling. She works with charms, spells, pentagrams and other trickery which is beyond our understanding. Come down, you witch, you hag, you; come down, I order you!*

MISTRESS FORD
Nay, good, sweet husband! Good gentlemen, let him
not strike the old woman.

*No, good sweet husband! Good gentleman, don't let him
hit the old woman.*

Re-enter FALSTAFF in woman's clothes, and MISTRESS PAGE

MISTRESS PAGE
Come, Mother Prat; come, give me your hand.

Come, Mother Prat; give me your hand.

FORD
I'll prat her.

I'll prat her.

Beating him

Out of my door, you witch, you hag, you baggage, you
polecat, you runyon! out, out! I'll conjure you,
I'll fortune-tell you.

Out of my house, you witch, you hack, you baggage, you
polecat, you bitch! Get out, out! I'll give you magic,
I'll tell your fortune.

Exit FALSTAFF

MISTRESS PAGE
Are you not ashamed? I think you have killed the
poor woman.

Aren't you ashamed? I think you have killed the
poor woman.

MISTRESS FORD
Nay, he will do it. 'Tis a goodly credit for you.

It looks like he will. There's a fine thing.

FORD
Hang her, witch!

Hang her, the witch!

SIR HUGH EVANS
By the yea and no, I think the 'oman is a witch
indeed: I like not when a 'oman has a great peard;
I spy a great peard under his muffler.

Well absolutely, I think the woman is certainly
a witch: I don't like it when a woman has a great
beard; I saw a great beard under his scarf.

FORD
Will you follow, gentlemen? I beseech you, follow;
see but the issue of my jealousy: if I cry out thus
upon no trail, never trust me when I open again.

Will you chase him, gentlemen? I beg you, chase;
come and see the result of my jealousy: if this
proves
to be a false scent, never trust me again when I call.

PAGE
Let's obey his humour a little further: come,
gentlemen.

Let's go along with him for a while longer: come
on, gentlemen.

Exeunt FORD, PAGE, SHALLOW, DOCTOR CAIUS, and SIR HUGH EVANS

MISTRESS PAGE
Trust me, he beat him most pitifully.

I swear, he beat him very pitifully.

MISTRESS FORD
Nay, by the mass, that he did not; he beat him most
unpitifully, methought.

Well I can swear that he didn't; he beat him most
unpitifully, I thought.

MISTRESS PAGE

I'll have the cudgel hallowed and hung o'er the altar; it hath done meritorious service.

MISTRESS FORD

What think you? may we, with the warrant of womanhood and the witness of a good conscience, pursue him with any further revenge?

MISTRESS PAGE

The spirit of wantonness is, sure, scared out of him: if the devil have him not in fee-simple, with fine and recovery, he will never, I think, in the way of waste, attempt us again.

MISTRESS FORD

Shall we tell our husbands how we have served him?

MISTRESS PAGE

Yes, by all means; if it be but to scrape the figures out of your husband's brains. If they can find in their hearts the poor unvirtuous fat knight shall be any further afflicted, we two will still be the ministers.

MISTRESS FORD

I'll warrant they'll have him publicly shamed: and methinks there would be no period to the jest, should he not be publicly shamed.

MISTRESS PAGE

Come, to the forge with it then; shape it: I would not have things cool.

Exeunt

I'll have the stick blessed and hung over the altar; it's done good work.

What do you think? May we, with the licence of womanhood and the witness of a clear conscience, take any more revenge on him?

*I think his lustful feelings have certainly been scared out of him: if the devil hasn't got him completely under his control,
with a watertight contract, he will never, I think, try his unlawful attempts on us again.*

Shall we tell our husbands what we did to him?

Yes, certainly; if nothing else to stop your husband imagining such things. If they decide that the poor badly behaved fat knight should have any more punishment, we two will still hand it out.

I'll bet they'll want him to be publicly shamed: and I don't think the joke will have a proper ending, unless he is publicly shamed.

Come on then, let's strike while the iron's hot: I don't want things to cool down.

SCENE III. A room in the Garter Inn.

Enter Host and BARDOLPH

BARDOLPH
Sir, the Germans desire to have three of your
horses: the duke himself will be to-morrow at
court, and they are going to meet him.

*Sir, those Germans want to have three of your
horses: the Duke himself will be at court
tomorrow and they are going to meet him.*

Host
What duke should that he comes so secretly? I hear
not of him in the court. Let me speak with the
gentlemen: they speak English?

*What sort of Duke is this that comes so secretly? I
haven't heard him spoken of at court. Let me speak
with the gentlemen: do they speak English?*

BARDOLPH
Ay, sir; I'll call them to you.

Yes, sir; I'll call them for you.

Host
They shall have my horses; but I'll make them pay;
I'll sauce them: they have had my house a week at
command; I have turned away my other guests: they
must come off; I'll sauce them. Come.

*They shall have my horses; but I'll make them pay;
I'll overcharge them: they have had my house to
themselves for a week; I have turned away my other
guests: they must
pay the price; I'll overcharge them. Come on.*

Exeunt

SCENE IV. A room in FORD'S house.

Enter PAGE, FORD, MISTRESS PAGE, MISTRESS FORD, and SIR HUGH EVANS

SIR HUGH EVANS
'Tis one of the best discretions of a 'oman as ever
I did look upon.

*It's one of the best descriptions of a woman
I have ever seen.*

PAGE
And did he send you both these letters at an instant?

And he sent you both these letters straight away?

MISTRESS PAGE
Within a quarter of an hour.

Within a quarter of an hour.

FORD
Pardon me, wife. Henceforth do what thou wilt;
I rather will suspect the sun with cold
Than thee with wantonness: now doth thy honour stand
In him that was of late an heretic,
As firm as faith.

*Forgive me, wife. From now on do what you want;
I would rather suspect the sun of being cold
than you of being unfaithful: I was an unbeliever,
now your honour is as solid to me as my faith.*

PAGE
'Tis well, 'tis well; no more:
Be not as extreme in submission
As in offence.
But let our plot go forward: let our wives
Yet once again, to make us public sport,
Appoint a meeting with this old fat fellow,
Where we may take him and disgrace him for it.

*Good, good; that's enough: don't go as overboard
in apologising as you did in offending.
But let's get on with our plan: let our wives
once again, for everybody's fun,
arrange a meeting with this old fat fellow
where we can grab him and humiliate him for it.*

FORD
There is no better way than that they spoke of.

There's no better plan than the one they mentioned.

PAGE
How? to send him word they'll meet him in the park
at midnight? Fie, fie! he'll never come.

*That one? To send him word that they'll meet him in the park
at midnight? Hogwash! He'll never come.*

SIR HUGH EVANS
You say he has been thrown in the rivers and has
been grievously peaten as an old 'oman: methinks
there should be terrors in him that he should not
come; methinks his flesh is punished, he shall have
no desires.

*You say he has been thrown in the river and has
been severely beaten as an old woman: I think
he will be too frightened to come;
I think his flesh has been punished, his lust
will have died.*

PAGE
So think I too.

I think so too.

MISTRESS FORD

Devise but how you'll use him when he comes,
And let us two devise to bring him thither.

MISTRESS PAGE
There is an old tale goes that Herne the hunter,
Sometime a keeper here in Windsor forest,
Doth all the winter-time, at still midnight,
Walk round about an oak, with great ragg'd horns;
And there he blasts the tree and takes the cattle
And makes milch-kine yield blood and shakes a
chain
In a most hideous and dreadful manner:
You have heard of such a spirit, and well you know
The superstitious idle-headed eld
Received and did deliver to our age
This tale of Herne the hunter for a truth.

PAGE
Why, yet there want not many that do fear
In deep of night to walk by this Herne's oak:
But what of this?

MISTRESS FORD
Marry, this is our device;
That Falstaff at that oak shall meet with us.

PAGE
Well, let it not be doubted but he'll come:
And in this shape when you have brought him
thither,
What shall be done with him? what is your plot?

MISTRESS PAGE
That likewise have we thought upon, and thus:
Nan Page my daughter and my little son
And three or four more of their growth we'll dress
Like urchins, ouphes and fairies, green and white,
With rounds of waxen tapers on their heads,
And rattles in their hands: upon a sudden,
As Falstaff, she and I, are newly met,
Let them from forth a sawpit rush at once
With some diffused song: upon their sight,
We two in great amazedness will fly:
Then let them all encircle him about
And, fairy-like, to-pinch the unclean knight,
And ask him why, that hour of fairy revel,
In their so sacred paths he dares to tread
In shape profane.

MISTRESS FORD

You just plan what you'll do with him when he
comes,
leave it to us to get him there.

There is an old story that Herne the Hunter,
who was once a gamekeeper in Windsor Forest,
in the winter, at the dead of midnight,
walks around an oak, with great shaggy horns;
he explodes trees and possesses the cattle
and makes the milk cows give blood and rattles a
chain
in a most hideous and dreadful manner:
you have heard of this spirit, and you well know
that the superstitious weak minded people of olden
times
swallowed this tale of Herne the Hunter and passed
it down to our times as being true.

Well, there are still many who are scared
to walk past Herne's oak in the depths of night:
but so what?

Well, this is our plan;
that Falstaff shall meet us at that oak.

Well, let's assume that he does come:
what will you do with him once you've
got him there, dressed as Herne as you order?
What's your plan?

We've thought of that as well, it's this:
Nan Page my daughter and my little son
and three or four more of their size we'll dress up
as urchins, elves and fairies, green and white,
with stubs of wax candles on their heads
and rattles in their hands: all of a sudden,
just as she and I meet Falstaff,
let them jump out of a hollow
singing some wild song; seeing them,
we two shall run away in fear;
then let them circle round him,
and pinch the dirty knight like fairies do,
and ask him why he dares to
walk upon their sacred paths in their
festival time, in such an unholy shape.

And till he tell the truth,
Let the supposed fairies pinch him sound
And burn him with their tapers.

MISTRESS PAGE
The truth being known,
We'll all present ourselves, dis-horn the spirit,
And mock him home to Windsor.

FORD
The children must
Be practised well to this, or they'll ne'er do't.

SIR HUGH EVANS
I will teach the children their behaviors; and I
will be like a jack-an-apes also, to burn the
knight with my taber.

FORD
That will be excellent. I'll go and buy them vizards.

MISTRESS PAGE
My Nan shall be the queen of all the fairies,
Finely attired in a robe of white.

PAGE
That silk will I go buy.

Aside

And in that time
Shall Master Slender steal my Nan away
And marry her at Eton. Go send to Falstaff straight.

FORD
Nay I'll to him again in name of Brook
He'll tell me all his purpose: sure, he'll come.

MISTRESS PAGE
Fear not you that. Go get us properties
And tricking for our fairies.

SIR HUGH EVANS
Let us about it: it is admirable pleasures and fery
honest knaveries.

Exeunt PAGE, FORD, and SIR HUGH EVANS

MISTRESS PAGE
Go, Mistress Ford,

And until he tells the truth,
let the pretend fairies pinch him hard
and burn him with their candles.

Once he's told the truth,
we'll all show ourselves, take off his horns,
and make fun of him all the way home to Windsor.

The children must be well drilled
in this, or they'll never get it right.

I will teach the children what to do; and I
will dress up as an evil spirit too, so I can burn
the knight with my candle.

That will do nicely. I'll go and buy them masks.

My Nan shall be the Queen of the fairies,
beautifully dressed in a white robe.

I will go and buy the silk for it.

And while I'm doing so
Master Slender will steal my Nan away
and marry her at Eton. Go and send for Falstaff at
once.

I'll go to him again disguised as Brook,
he'll tell me all his plans: he'll definitely come.

Don't you worry about that. Go and get us props
and costumes for our fairies.

Let's do it: it's great fun and very
honest trickery.

Go, Mistress Ford,

Send quickly to Sir John, to know his mind.

Exit MISTRESS FORD

I'll to the doctor: he hath my good will,
And none but he, to marry with Nan Page.
That Slender, though well landed, is an idiot;
And he my husband best of all affects.
The doctor is well money'd, and his friends
Potent at court: he, none but he, shall have her,
Though twenty thousand worthier come to crave
her.

Exit

send a message to Sir John at once, to see what he's thinking.

I'll write to the doctor: he's the one I favour, no one but him, to marry Nan Page. That Slender, though he has plenty of property, is an idiot; he's the one my husband favours most of all. The doctor is rich, and his friends are influential at court: he, and no other, shall have her, even if twenty thousand better men came to ask for her.

SCENE V. A room in the Garter Inn.

Enter Host and SIMPLE

Host
What wouldst thou have, boor? what: thick-skin?
speak, breathe, discuss; brief, short, quick, snap.

SIMPLE
Marry, sir, I come to speak with Sir John Falstaff
from Master Slender.

Host
There's his chamber, his house, his castle, his
standing-bed and truckle-bed; 'tis painted about
with the story of the Prodigal, fresh and new. Go
knock and call; he'll speak like an
Anthropophaginian
unto thee: knock, I say.

SIMPLE
There's an old woman, a fat woman, gone up into
his
chamber: I'll be so bold as stay, sir, till she come
down; I come to speak with her, indeed.

Host
Ha! a fat woman! the knight may be robbed: I'll
call. Bully knight! bully Sir John! speak from
thy lungs military: art thou there? it is thine
host, thine Ephesian, calls.

FALSTAFF
[Above] How now, mine host!

Host
Here's a Bohemian-Tartar tarries the coming down
of
thy fat woman. Let her descend, bully, let her
descend; my chambers are honourable: fie! privacy?
fie!

Enter FALSTAFF

FALSTAFF
There was, mine host, an old fat woman even now
with

me; but she's gone.

What do you want, you cad? What, you clod?
Come on, spit it out and make it snappy.

Why, sir, I have come from Master Slender to speak
with Sir John Falstaff.

There's his bedroom, his house, his castle, his
main bed and daybed; the hangings are all painted
with the story of the prodigal son, freshly done.
You go and knock and call for him; he'll treat you
like a cannibal: go on, knock.

There's an old woman, a fat woman, who went up
into
his room: I think that I will wait, sir, until she
comes back down; in fact I've come to speak with
her.

Ha! A fat woman! The knight may be robbed: I'll
call. Good knight! Good Sir John! Give us one of
your parade ground shouts: are you there? This is
your landlord, your good friend, calling.

Hello there, mine host!

There is a savage here waiting for your fat woman
to come down. Let her come down, old man, let her
come down; this is a respectable place: no secret
goings-on here!

Landlord, I did have an old fat woman with me
just now; but she's gone.

SIMPLE
Pray you, sir, was't not the wise woman of
Brentford?

FALSTAFF
Ay, marry, was it, mussel-shell: what would you
with her?

SIMPLE
My master, sir, Master Slender, sent to her, seeing
her go through the streets, to know, sir, whether
one Nym, sir, that beguiled him of a chain, had the
chain or no.

FALSTAFF
I spake with the old woman about it.

SIMPLE
And what says she, I pray, sir?

FALSTAFF
Marry, she says that the very same man that
beguiled Master Slender of his chain cozened him
of
it.

SIMPLE
I would I could have spoken with the woman
herself;
I had other things to have spoken with her too from
him.

FALSTAFF
What are they? let us know.

Host
Ay, come; quick.

SIMPLE
I may not reveal them, sir.

Host
Reveal them, or thou diest.

SIMPLE
Why, sir, they were nothing but about Mistress
Anne
Page; to know if it were my master's fortune to
have her or no.

*Excuse me, sir, wasn't it the wise woman of
Brentford?*

*Yes, certainly, it was, you gaping fool: what do you
want with her?*

*My master, sir, Master Slender, enquired after her,
seeing
her walk through the streets; he wanted to know,
sir, whether a man called Nym, sir, that tricked him
out of a chain, had the chain or not.*

I spoke to the old woman about it.

Please can you tell me what she says, sir?

*Well, she says that the same man who
tricked Master Slender out of his chain stole
it from him.*

*I wish I could have spoken with the woman herself;
there were other things he wanted me to ask.*

What are they? Tell us.

Yes come on, tell us.

I can't disclose them, sir.

Disclose them or you're dead.

*Well, sir, they were only about Mistress Anne
Page; my master wanted to know if it was his fate
to have her or not.*

FALSTAFF
'Tis, 'tis his fortune.

Yes it is, it is his fate.

SIMPLE
What, sir?

What, sir?

FALSTAFF
To have her, or no. Go; say the woman told me so.

To have her, or not. Go on, tell him the woman told me so.

SIMPLE
May I be bold to say so, sir?

Dare I say this?

FALSTAFF
Ay, sir; like who more bold.

Yes, sir; be as bold as you like.

SIMPLE
I thank your worship: I shall make my master glad with these tidings.

Thank you your worship: this news will make my master glad.

Exit

Host
Thou art clerkly, thou art clerkly, Sir John. Was there a wise woman with thee?

You're a scholar, a scholar, Sir John. Was there a wise woman with you?

FALSTAFF
Ay, that there was, mine host; one that hath taught me more wit than ever I learned before in my life; and I paid nothing for it neither, but was paid for my learning.

Yes there was, landlord; one who taught me more sense than I have ever learned in my life; and I didn't pay for it either, but was paid for learning.

Enter BARDOLPH

BARDOLPH
Out, alas, sir! cozenage, mere cozenage!

Oh, alas, sir! Cheating, straightforward cheating!

Host
Where be my horses? speak well of them, varletto.

Where are my horses? You'd better give me good news, scoundrel.

BARDOLPH
Run away with the cozeners; for so soon as I came beyond Eton, they threw me off from behind one of them, in a slough of mire; and set spurs and away, like three German devils, three Doctor Faustuses.

Gone with the cheaters; for as soon as we got past Eton they threw me off from where I sat behind one of them, into the mud; they dug in their spurs and set off, like three German devils, three Dr Faustuses.

Host
They are gone but to meet the duke, villain: do not say they be fled; Germans are honest men.

They've only gone to meet the Duke, scoundrel; don't say that they've bolted; Germans are honest men.

Enter SIR HUGH EVANS

SIR HUGH EVANS
Where is mine host?

Host
What is the matter, sir?

SIR HUGH EVANS
Have a care of your entertainments: there is a
friend of mine come to town tells me there is three
cozen-germans that has cozened all the hosts of
Readins, of Maidenhead, of Colebrook, of horses
and
money. I tell you for good will, look you: you
are wise and full of gibes and vlouting-stocks, and
'tis not convenient you should be cozened. Fare you
well.

Exit

Enter DOCTOR CAIUS

DOCTOR CAIUS
Vere is mine host de Jarteer?

Host
Here, master doctor, in perplexity and doubtful
dilemma.

DOCTOR CAIUS
I cannot tell vat is dat: but it is tell-a me dat
you make grand preparation for a duke de Jamany:
by
my trot, dere is no duke dat the court is know to
come. I tell you for good vill: adieu.

Exit

Host
Hue and cry, villain, go! Assist me, knight. I am
undone! Fly, run, hue and cry, villain! I am undone!

Exeunt Host and BARDOLPH

FALSTAFF
I would all the world might be cozened; for I have
been cozened and beaten too. If it should come to
the ear of the court, how I have been transformed
and how my transformation hath been washed and
cudgelled, they would melt me out of my fat drop
by

Where is the landlord?

What's the matter, sir?

*Be careful who you welcome in: a friend
of mine has come to town and tells me that there are
three
fake Germans who have conned all the landlords of
Reading, Maidenhead and Colebrook out of horses
and money. I tell you as a goodwill gesture, you
note: you
are smart and full of jokes and mockery, but
you shouldn't be conned. Goodbye.*

Where is the landlord of the Garter?

Here, master doctor, worried and confused.

*I don't know what you're talking about: but I have
been told
that you are making great preparations to welcome
a German duke: upon my word, no such duke is
expected at court. I tell you this out of goodwill:
goodbye.*

*Raise the alarm, you scoundrel! Help me, knight. I
am tricked! Hurry, run and raise the alarm, you
scoundrel! I am tricked!*

*I wish all the world could be tricked; for I have
been tricked and beaten as well. If the court should
get to
hear about how I have been changed
and how in the process I have been soaked and
beaten, they would melt me down for fat*

drop and liquor fishermen's boots with me; I warrant
they would whip me with their fine wits till I were as crest-fallen as a dried pear. I never prospered since I forswore myself at primero. Well, if my wind were but long enough to say my prayers, I would repent.

and grease fisherman's boots with me; I guarantee they would beat me with their great wits until I was as shrivelled as a dried pear. I never have had any luck since I cheated at cards. Well, if I had enough breath to do it, I would repent.

Enter MISTRESS QUICKLY

Now, whence come you?

Now, where have you come from?

MISTRESS QUICKLY
From the two parties, forsooth.

Why, from the two ladies.

FALSTAFF
The devil take one party and his dam the other! and so they shall be both bestowed. I have suffered more
for their sakes, more than the villanous inconstancy of man's disposition is able to bear.

*The devil take one of them and his mother the other! That will take care of them both. I have suffered more
for their sakes than the useless weakness of man is able to bear.*

MISTRESS QUICKLY
And have not they suffered? Yes, I warrant; speciously one of them; Mistress Ford, good heart, is beaten black and blue, that you cannot see a white spot about her.

And haven't they suffered? They certainly have, especially one of them; Mistress Ford, my dear, has been beaten black and blue, so you can't see an inch of white skin.

FALSTAFF
What tellest thou me of black and blue? I was beaten myself into all the colours of the rainbow; and I was like to be apprehended for the witch of Brentford: but that my admirable dexterity of wit, my counterfeiting the action of an old woman, delivered me, the knave constable had set me i' the stocks, i' the common stocks, for a witch.

Who cares about black and blue? I was beaten all the colours of the rainbow; it seemed I was going to be arrested for being the witch of Brentford: if it hadn't been for my admirable quick-wittedness, impersonating an old woman, the rascally constable would have put me in the stocks, in the common stocks, as a witch.

MISTRESS QUICKLY
Sir, let me speak with you in your chamber: you shall hear how things go; and, I warrant, to your content. Here is a letter will say somewhat. Good hearts, what ado here is to bring you together! Sure, one of you does not serve heaven well, that you are so crossed.

Sir, let me speak with you in your room: I shall tell you how things stand; I promise you will be pleased to hear it. Here is a letter which explains a little. My dears, how difficult it is to bring you together! I'm sure one of you must have upset heaven for things to be so awkward.

FALSTAFF
Come up into my chamber.

Come up to my room.

Exeunt

SCENE VI. Another room in the Garter Inn.

Enter FENTON and Host

Host
Master Fenton, talk not to me; my mind is heavy: I
will give over all.

FENTON
Yet hear me speak. Assist me in my purpose,
And, as I am a gentleman, I'll give thee
A hundred pound in gold more than your loss.

Host
I will hear you, Master Fenton; and I will at the
least keep your counsel.

FENTON
From time to time I have acquainted you
With the dear love I bear to fair Anne Page;
Who mutually hath answer'd my affection,
So far forth as herself might be her chooser,
Even to my wish: I have a letter from her
Of such contents as you will wonder at;
The mirth whereof so larded with my matter,
That neither singly can be manifested,
Without the show of both; fat Falstaff
Hath a great scene: the image of the jest
I'll show you here at large. Hark, good mine host.
To-night at Herne's oak, just 'twixt twelve and one,
Must my sweet Nan present the Fairy Queen;
The purpose why, is here: in which disguise,
While other jests are something rank on foot,
Her father hath commanded her to slip
Away with Slender and with him at Eton
Immediately to marry: she hath consented: Now,
sir,
Her mother, ever strong against that match
And firm for Doctor Caius, hath appointed
That he shall likewise shuffle her away,
While other sports are tasking of their minds,
And at the deanery, where a priest attends,
Straight marry her: to this her mother's plot
She seemingly obedient likewise hath
Made promise to the doctor. Now, thus it rests:
Her father means she shall be all in white,
And in that habit, when Slender sees his time
To take her by the hand and bid her go,
She shall go with him: her mother hath intended,

Master Fenton, don't talk to me; I'm depressed; I
give up.

Just listen to me. Help me with my plans,
and I swear as I am a gentleman that I'll make up
your losses and give you a hundred pounds in gold
on top.

I will listen to you, Master Fenton; and I will
at least keep your secrets.

From time to time I have told you about
the dear love I have for beautiful Anne Page,
who in as much as she can make her own choice
has returned my affection as well
as I could wish for. I have a letter from her,
the contents of which will amaze you,
the joke of which is so mixed up with my affair
that I can't tell you about one
without the other. Fat Falstaff
plays a great part; I will outline the
idea of the joke for you. Listen, my good landlord.
Tonight at Herne's oak, just between twelve and
one, my sweet Nan will appear as the Fairy Queen–
this explains why–and in this disguise,
whilst other jokes are afoot,
her father has ordered her to slip
away with Slender, and to marry him at once
at Eton; she has agreed.
Now, sir, her mother, who is very much against that
match and favours Doctor Caius, has arranged
that he too should steal her away,
while other matters keep people distracted,
and go to the chapel, where a priest is waiting,
and marry her once; she has pretended
to be obedient to this plot of her mother's as well
and made a promise to the Doctor. Now, this is how
it stands: her father intends for her to be dressed all
in white; in that dress, when Slender sees the
opportunity
to take her by the hand and tell her to go,
she shall go with him; her mother intends,

The better to denote her to the doctor,
For they must all be mask'd and vizarded,
That quaint in green she shall be loose enrobed,
With ribands pendent, flaring 'bout her head;
And when the doctor spies his vantage ripe,
To pinch her by the hand, and, on that token,
The maid hath given consent to go with him.

Host
Which means she to deceive, father or mother?

FENTON
Both, my good host, to go along with me:
And here it rests, that you'll procure the vicar
To stay for me at church 'twixt twelve and one,
And, in the lawful name of marrying,
To give our hearts united ceremony.

Host
Well, husband your device; I'll to the vicar:
Bring you the maid, you shall not lack a priest.

FENTON
So shall I evermore be bound to thee;
Besides, I'll make a present recompense.

Exeunt

in order to mark her out better for the Doctor–
for they will all be wearing masks and face
coverings– that she will be neatly dressed in green,
with ribbons hanging down around her head;
and when the Doctor sees his opportunity,
to grab her by the hand, that will be the sign
on which the girl has agreed to go with him.

Who does she mean to deceive, her father or her
mother?

Both, good landlord, so that she can come with me:
and what I want is for you to get the vicar
to wait for me at the church between twelve and
one, so that our hearts can be joined together
in the lawful name of matrimony.

Well, you do your part; I'll go to the vicar:
if you produce the girl, you won't lack the priest.

I shall be indebted to you for ever;
and also, I'll reward you at once.

Act 5

SCENE I. A room in the Garter Inn.

Enter FALSTAFF and MISTRESS QUICKLY

FALSTAFF
Prithee, no more prattling; go. I'll hold. This is
the third time; I hope good luck lies in odd
numbers. Away I go. They say there is divinity in
odd numbers, either in nativity, chance, or death.
Away!

MISTRESS QUICKLY
I'll provide you a chain; and I'll do what I can to
get you a pair of horns.

FALSTAFF
Away, I say; time wears: hold up your head, and
mince.

Exit MISTRESS QUICKLY

Enter FORD
How now, Master Brook! Master Brook, the matter
will be known to-night, or never. Be you in the
Park about midnight, at Herne's oak, and you shall
see wonders.

FORD
Went you not to her yesterday, sir, as you told me
you had appointed?

FALSTAFF
I went to her, Master Brook, as you see, like a poor
old man: but I came from her, Master Brook, like a
poor old woman. That same knave Ford, her
husband,
hath the finest mad devil of jealousy in him,
Master Brook, that ever governed frenzy. I will tell
you: he beat me grievously, in the shape of a
woman; for in the shape of man, Master Brook, I
fear
not Goliath with a weaver's beam; because I know
also life is a shuttle. I am in haste; go along
with me: I'll tell you all, Master Brook. Since I
plucked geese, played truant and whipped top, I
knew
not what 'twas to be beaten till lately. Follow
me: I'll tell you strange things of this knave
Ford, on whom to-night I will be revenged, and I

Please, no more chatter; go. I'll be there. This is
the third time; I hope good luck comes with odd
numbers. Off I go. They say that there is fate
in odd numbers, in birth, luck or death. Go!

I'll get you a chain; and I'll do what I can to
get you a pair of horns.

Go, I say; time is passing: lift up your head and trot
off.

Hello there, Master Brook! Master Brook, the thing
will be decided tonight or never. Be in the
Park about midnight, at Herne's oak, and you shall
see amazing things.

Didn't you go to see her yesterday, sir, as you told
me you had arranged?

I went to see her, Master Brook, as you see me now,
a poor old man: but I came away, Master Brook,
like a poor old woman. That rascal Ford, her
husband,
has the most amazing angry jealous daemon in him,
Master Brook, that ever drove a man mad. I will tell
you: he beat me very roughly, when I was disguised
as a woman; when I am a man, Master Brook, I
wouldn't be afraid
of Goliath armed with a tree trunk, because I know
that life is fragile as a twig. I'm in a hurry; come
along with me: I'll tell you all about it, Master
Brook. I haven't experienced such a beating since
I was a naughty schoolboy. Follow me: I'll tell you
strange things about this rascal Ford, on whom I
will get my revenge tonight. Come with me. Strange
things are afoot, Master Brooke! Come with me.

will deliver his wife into your hand. Follow.
Strange things in hand, Master Brook! Follow.

Exeunt

*I shall be indebted to you for ever;
and also, I'll reward you at once.*

SCENE II. Windsor Park.

Enter PAGE, SHALLOW, and SLENDER

PAGE
Come, come; we'll couch i' the castle-ditch till we
see the light of our fairies. Remember, son Slender,
my daughter.

*Come on; we'll hide in the castle moat until we
see the light of our fairies. Remember, Slender my
son, my daughter.*

SLENDER
Ay, forsooth; I have spoke with her and we have a
nay-word how to know one another: I come to her
in
white, and cry 'mum;' she cries 'budget;' and by
that we know one another.

*Yes, indeed; I have spoken to her and we have a
password to recognise each other with: I will come
to her (she'll be in
white) and say 'mum;' she will say ' budget;' and
that will let us know who we are.*

SHALLOW
That's good too: but what needs either your 'mum'
or her 'budget?' the white will decipher her well
enough. It hath struck ten o'clock.

*That's a good plan: but why do you need to say
'mum' or her say 'budget'? Her white clothes will
show her well enough. It's gone ten o'clock.*

PAGE
The night is dark; light and spirits will become it
well. Heaven prosper our sport! No man means evil
but the devil, and we shall know him by his horns.
Let's away; follow me.

*It's a dark night; lights and ghosts will suit it
well. May heaven help our joke! No man means
evil, just the devil, and we shall recognise him by
his horns. Let's go; follow me.*

Exeunt

SCENE III. A street leading to the Park.

Enter MISTRESS PAGE, MISTRESS FORD, and DOCTOR CAIUS

MISTRESS PAGE
Master doctor, my daughter is in green: when you
see your time, take her by the hand, away with her
to the deanery, and dispatch it quickly. Go before
into the Park: we two must go together.

DOCTOR CAIUS
I know vat I have to do. Adieu.

MISTRESS PAGE
Fare you well, sir.

Exit DOCTOR CAIUS

My husband will not rejoice so much at the abuse of
Falstaff as he will chafe at the doctor's marrying
my daughter: but 'tis no matter; better a little
chiding than a great deal of heart-break.

MISTRESS FORD
Where is Nan now and her troop of fairies, and the
Welsh devil Hugh?

MISTRESS PAGE
They are all couched in a pit hard by Herne's oak,
with obscured lights; which, at the very instant of
Falstaff's and our meeting, they will at once
display to the night.

MISTRESS FORD
That cannot choose but amaze him.

MISTRESS PAGE
If he be not amazed, he will be mocked; if he be
amazed, he will every way be mocked.

MISTRESS FORD
We'll betray him finely.

MISTRESS PAGE
Against such lewdsters and their lechery
Those that betray them do no treachery.

MISTRESS FORD
The hour draws on. To the oak, to the oak!

Master doctor, my daughter is dressed in green:
when you see the opportunity, take her by the hand,
go with her to the chapel, and get the business done
quickly. Go ahead
into the park: we two must go together.

I know what I have to do. Goodbye.

Good luck, sir.

My husband will not be as happy at tormenting
Falstaff as he will be angry with the doctor
marrying my daughter: but never mind; better a
little telling off than a great deal of heartbreak.

Where is Nan now and the troop of fairies, and the
Welsh devil Hugh?

They are all hidden in a hollow right by Herne's
oak,
with shaded lights; as soon as we meet
Falstaff they will let them blaze into the night.

That can't help but astonish him.

If it doesn't bewilder him, he will be mocked; if he is
bewildered, he will be even more mocked.

We'll set him up nicely.

When dealing with such rude men and their lechery
it's no treachery to expose them.

The time is coming near. Let's get to the oak!

Exeunt

SCENE IV. Another part of the Park.

Enter FALSTAFF disguised as Herne

FALSTAFF
The Windsor bell hath struck twelve; the minute
draws on. Now, the hot-blooded gods assist me!
Remember, Jove, thou wast a bull for thy Europa;
love
set on thy horns. O powerful love! that, in some
respects, makes a beast a man, in some other, a man
a beast. You were also, Jupiter, a swan for the love
of Leda. O omnipotent Love! how near the god
drew
to the complexion of a goose! A fault done first in
the form of a beast. O Jove, a beastly fault! And
then another fault in the semblance of a fowl; think
on 't, Jove; a foul fault! When gods have hot
backs, what shall poor men do? For me, I am here a
Windsor stag; and the fattest, I think, i' the
forest. Send me a cool rut-time, Jove, or who can
blame me to piss my tallow? Who comes here? my
doe?

Enter MISTRESS FORD and MISTRESS PAGE

MISTRESS FORD
Sir John! art thou there, my deer? my male deer?

FALSTAFF
My doe with the black scut! Let the sky rain
potatoes; let it thunder to the tune of Green
Sleeves, hail kissing-comfits and snow eringoes; let
there come a tempest of provocation, I will shelter
me here.

MISTRESS FORD
Mistress Page is come with me, sweetheart.

FALSTAFF
Divide me like a bribe buck, each a haunch: I will
keep my sides to myself, my shoulders for the
fellow
of this walk, and my horns I bequeath your
husbands.
Am I a woodman, ha? Speak I like Herne the
hunter?

*The clock at Windsor has struck twelve; the time
is coming near. Now, may the lusty gods assist me!
Remember, Jupiter, you became a bull for your
Europa; you aimed at love with your horns. Oh
powerful love that sometimes
can make an animal into a man; at other times it
makes a man an animal. You were also, Jupiter, a
swan for the love of Leda. Oh all-powerful love,
how nearly the God became
the goose! It was a sin first done in the
shape of a beast: O Jupiter, a beastly sin! And then
another sin when you were shaped like a fowl: think
of it, Jupiter, a foul sin! When even gods get lustful,
what shall poor men do? As for me, here I am, a
Windsor stag, and I think I'm the fattest in the
forest. Please make my mating season cool, Jupiter,
or I swear my fat will melt.
Who is this coming? My mate?*

Why, now is Cupid a child of conscience; he makes
restitution. As I am a true spirit, welcome!

Sir John! Are you there, my dear? My buck?

My doe with the black tail! Let the sky rain potatoes; let the thunder play the tune of Greensleeves, let the hail be breath fresheners and the snow aphrodisiacs; let there be a storm of temptation, I will shelter here.

Mistress Page has come with me, sweetheart.

Split me between you like a poached deer, a haunch each: I will take my sides for myself, give the gamekeeper my shoulders and your husbands can have the horns. Am I a hunter, eh? Do I speak like Herne the hunter? Why, Cupid is showing that he has a conscience; he's making up for the past. Welcome from a faithful spirit!

Noise within

MISTRESS PAGE
Alas, what noise?

Oh no, what's that noise?

MISTRESS FORD
Heaven forgive our sins!

May heaven forgive our sins!

FALSTAFF
What should this be?

What's going on?

MISTRESS FORD MISTRESS PAGE

Away, away!
They run off

Run, run!

FALSTAFF
I think the devil will not have me damned, lest the
oil that's in me should set hell on fire; he would
never else cross me thus.

*I don't think the devil wants me to be dammed, in
case the oil inside me sets hell on fire; so he is
stopping my fun on earth.*

**Enter SIR HUGH EVANS, disguised as before; PISTOL, as Hobgoblin; MISTRESS QUICKLY,
ANNE PAGE, and others, as Fairies, with tapers**

MISTRESS QUICKLY
Fairies, black, grey, green, and white,
You moonshine revellers and shades of night,
You orphan heirs of fixed destiny,
Attend your office and your quality.
Crier Hobgoblin, make the fairy oyes.

*Fairies, black, grey, green and white,
you dancers in the moonshine and ghosts of night,
you solitary performers of your duties,
attend to your professions.
Crier hobgoblin, make the fairy announcement.*

PISTOL
Elves, list your names; silence, you airy toys.
Cricket, to Windsor chimneys shalt thou leap:
Where fires thou find'st unraked and hearths
unswept,
There pinch the maids as blue as bilberry:
Our radiant queen hates sluts and sluttery.

*Elves, answer the register; quiet, you airy beings.
Cricket, you shall inspect the chimneys of Windsor:
when you find fires unranked and hearths unswept,
pinch the maids until they are blue as bilberries;
our shining Queen hates slack girls and laziness.*

FALSTAFF
They are fairies; he that speaks to them shall die:
I'll wink and couch: no man their works must eye.

*They are fairies; anyone who speaks to them will
die: I'll close my eyes and hide: no man must look
on their works.*

Lies down upon his face

SIR HUGH EVANS
Where's Bede? Go you, and where you find a maid
That, ere she sleep, has thrice her prayers said,
Raise up the organs of her fantasy;
Sleep she as sound as careless infancy:

*Where's Bede? You go, and when you find a girl
who has said her prayers three times before bed,
give her sweet dreams;
she can sleep as soundly as a carefree baby:*

But those as sleep and think not on their sins,
Pinch them, arms, legs, backs, shoulders, sides and
shins.

MISTRESS QUICKLY
About, about;
Search Windsor Castle, elves, within and out:
Strew good luck, ouphes, on every sacred room:
That it may stand till the perpetual doom,
In state as wholesome as in state 'tis fit,
Worthy the owner, and the owner it.
The several chairs of order look you scour
With juice of balm and every precious flower:
Each fair instalment, coat, and several crest,
With loyal blazon, evermore be blest!
And nightly, meadow-fairies, look you sing,
Like to the Garter's compass, in a ring:
The expressure that it bears, green let it be,
More fertile-fresh than all the field to see;
And 'Honi soit qui mal y pense' write
In emerald tufts, flowers purple, blue and white;
Let sapphire, pearl and rich embroidery,
Buckled below fair knighthood's bending knee:
Fairies use flowers for their charactery.
Away; disperse: but till 'tis one o'clock,
Our dance of custom round about the oak
Of Herne the hunter, let us not forget.

SIR HUGH EVANS
Pray you, lock hand in hand; yourselves in order set
And twenty glow-worms shall our lanterns be,
To guide our measure round about the tree.
But, stay; I smell a man of middle-earth.

FALSTAFF
Heavens defend me from that Welsh fairy, lest he
transform me to a piece of cheese!

PISTOL
Vile worm, thou wast o'erlook'd even in thy birth.

MISTRESS QUICKLY
With trial-fire touch me his finger-end:
If he be chaste, the flame will back descend
And turn him to no pain; but if he start,
It is the flesh of a corrupted heart.

PISTOL
A trial, come.

---

*but those who go to sleep without thinking of their
sins, pinch them, arms, legs, backs, shoulders, sides
and shins.*

*Come on, come on,
search through Windsor Castle, elves, inside and
out; throw good luck, fairies, into every sacred
room so that it can stand until Judgement Day
in as healthy condition as suits its dignity,
deserving the owner, and the owner deserving it;
polish the chairs of the Knights of the Garter
with the juice of every scented flower and tree;
every fair seat, coat of arms, and different crests,
should be blessed, as well as their banners;
and every night, meadow fairies, you should sing,
in a circle like the symbol of the Garter:
let the impression it makes in the grass be green,
more fertile than the rest of the field; and
write, 'Evil be to him who evil thinks'
in green tufts, purple, blue and white flowers,
like the sapphire, pearl and rich embroidery
that the knight has on his garter:
fairies use flowers as their typeface.
Go to your work; but until it is one o'clock,
don't let us forget our traditional dance
around the oak of Herne the Hunter.*

*Now please join hands; put yourselves in order
and our lanterns shall be twenty glowworms,
to lead our dance around the tree.
But wait; I can smell a mortal man.*

*God save me from that Welsh fairy, in case he
should change me into a piece of cheese!*

*You vile worm, you were destined for evil from
birth.*

*Let me touch his fingertip with a testing flame:
if he is chaste, the flame will die down
and give him no pain; but if he flinches,
that proves he has a corrupted heart.*

A trial, let's do it.

SIR HUGH EVANS
Come, will this wood take fire?

Let's see, will this wood catch fire?

They burn him with their tapers

FALSTAFF
Oh, Oh, Oh!

Oh, oh, oh!

MISTRESS QUICKLY
Corrupt, corrupt, and tainted in desire!
About him, fairies; sing a scornful rhyme;
And, as you trip, still pinch him to your time.
SONG.
Fie on sinful fantasy!
Fie on lust and luxury!
Lust is but a bloody fire,
Kindled with unchaste desire,
Fed in heart, whose flames aspire
As thoughts do blow them, higher and higher.
Pinch him, fairies, mutually;
Pinch him for his villany;
Pinch him, and burn him, and turn him about,
Till candles and starlight and moonshine be out.

Corrupt, corrupt, and with filthy desires!
Dance round him fairies; sing a mocking song;
and as you skip, pinch him to the rhythm.

Away with sinful fantasy,
enough of lust and luxury!
Lust is just a fire in the blood,
lit with impure desires,
burning in the heart, whose flames reach,
as they are fanned by thoughts, higher and higher.
All of you fairies pinch him;
pinch him for his villainy;
pinch him, and burn him, and spin him round,
until the candles and the starlight and the
moonshine burn out.

During this song they pinch FALSTAFF. DOCTOR CAIUS comes one way, and steals away a boy in green; SLENDER another way, and takes off a boy in white; and FENTON comes and steals away ANN PAGE. A noise of hunting is heard within. All the Fairies run away. FALSTAFF pulls off his buck's head, and rises

Enter PAGE, FORD, MISTRESS PAGE, and MISTRESS FORD

PAGE
Nay, do not fly; I think we have watch'd you now.
Will none but Herne the hunter serve your turn?

No, do not run; I think we have trapped you now.
Will only Herne the Hunter do for you?

MISTRESS PAGE
I pray you, come, hold up the jest no higher.
Now, good Sir John, how like you Windsor wives?
See you these, husband? do not these fair yokes
Become the forest better than the town?

Please, come along, don't carry on the joke any
further. Now, good Sir John, what do you think of
the wives of Windsor? Do you see these horns,
husband? Don't these lovely things
look better in the forest than in the town?

FORD
Now, sir, who's a cuckold now? Master Brook,
Falstaff's a knave, a cuckoldly knave; here are his
horns, Master Brook: and, Master Brook, he hath
enjoyed nothing of Ford's but his buck-basket, his
cudgel, and twenty pounds of money, which must
be
paid to Master Brook; his horses are arrested for

Now, sir, who is a cuckold with horns now? Master
Brook, Falstaff's a knave, a cuckoldly knave; here
are his horns, Master Brook: and, Master Brook, he
has enjoyed nothing of Ford's except his laundry
basket, his stick, and twenty pounds in cash, which
he must
pay to Master Brook; his horses are being held in

it, Master Brook.

MISTRESS FORD
Sir John, we have had ill luck; we could never meet.
I will never take you for my love again; but I will
always count you my deer.

FALSTAFF
I do begin to perceive that I am made an ass.

FORD
Ay, and an ox too: both the proofs are extant.

FALSTAFF
And these are not fairies? I was three or four
times in the thought they were not fairies: and yet
the guiltiness of my mind, the sudden surprise of
my
powers, drove the grossness of the foppery into a
received belief, in despite of the teeth of all
rhyme and reason, that they were fairies. See now
how wit may be made a Jack-a-Lent, when 'tis upon
ill employment!

SIR HUGH EVANS
Sir John Falstaff, serve Got, and leave your
desires, and fairies will not pinse you.

FORD
Well said, fairy Hugh.

SIR HUGH EVANS
And leave your jealousies too, I pray you.

FORD
I will never mistrust my wife again till thou art
able to woo her in good English.

FALSTAFF
Have I laid my brain in the sun and dried it, that
it wants matter to prevent so gross o'erreaching as
this? Am I ridden with a Welsh goat too? shall I
have a coxcomb of frize? 'Tis time I were choked
with a piece of toasted cheese.

SIR HUGH EVANS
Seese is not good to give putter; your belly is all
putter.

FALSTAFF

lieu of payment, Master Brook.

*Sir John, we had bad luck; we never managed to
meet. I will never have you as my lover; but I will
always think of you as my deer.*

I begin to see that you've made an ass of me.

Yes and an ox too: the proof is here, quite plain.

*And these are not fairies? I suspected it
three or four times: and yet
with my guilty mind, and the sudden shock to my
senses, the silly fantasy became reality and
in spite of all rhyme or reason I believed they were
fairies.
See how fun can be made of a Halloween pumpkin,
when he's up to no good.*

*Sir John Falstaff, serve God, put aside your
desires, and the fairies will not pinch you.*

Well said, fairy Hugh.

And you lay off your jealousies, please.

*I will never mistrust my wife again until you can
chat her up in good English.*

*Have I put my brain out and shrivelled it in the sun,
so that I'm not clever enough to stop such a terrible
defeat as this? Am I teased by a Welsh goat too?
Shall I wear a Welsh jester's cap? It's time I was
choked with a piece of toasted cheese.*

*You shouldn't have butter with it, your belly is all
butter.*

'Seese' and 'putter'! have I lived to stand at the taunt of one that makes fritters of English? This is enough to be the decay of lust and late-walking through the realm.

MISTRESS PAGE
Why Sir John, do you think, though we would have the
virtue out of our hearts by the head and shoulders and have given ourselves without scruple to hell, that ever the devil could have made you our delight?

FORD
What, a hodge-pudding? a bag of flax?

MISTRESS PAGE
A puffed man?

PAGE
Old, cold, withered and of intolerable entrails?

FORD
And one that is as slanderous as Satan?

PAGE
And as poor as Job?

FORD
And as wicked as his wife?

SIR HUGH EVANS
And given to fornications, and to taverns and sack and wine and metheglins, and to drinkings and swearings and starings, pribbles and prabbles?

FALSTAFF
Well, I am your theme: you have the start of me; I am dejected; I am not able to answer the Welsh flannel; ignorance itself is a plummet o'er me: use me as you will.

FORD
Marry, sir, we'll bring you to Windsor, to one Master Brook, that you have cozened of money, to whom you should have been a pander: over and above
that you have suffered, I think to repay that money will be a biting affliction.

'Seese' and 'putter'! Have I sunk so low I can be mocked by someone who murders the English language? This should be enough to put down lust and late nights throughout the kingdom.

Why Sir John, do you think that even if we threw away all our virtues and gave ourselves unconditionally to hell that the devil would have ever made us want you?

What, a blood sausage? A sack of oily seeds?

A puffed up man?

Old, cold, withered and with a revolting stomach?

And one who is as big a liar as Satan?

And as poor as Job?

And as wicked as his wife?

And devoted to fornication, taverns, sherry, wine, mead, drinking, swearing, ogling, chatter and gossip?

Well, I am the butt of your jokes: you have the whip hand; I am cast down; I am not able to reply to the Welsh blabbermouth; stupidity is many levels above me: do what you want with me.

Well, sir, we'll take you to Windsor, to see Master Brook, that you cheated out of money, whom you were supposed to pimp for: over and above what you have suffered, I think it will sting you to repay that money.

PAGE
Yet be cheerful, knight: thou shalt eat a posset
to-night at my house; where I will desire thee to
laugh at my wife, that now laughs at thee: tell her
Master Slender hath married her daughter.

*But cheer up, knight: you shall eat a posset
tonight at my house; and there I will ask you to
laugh at my wife, who now laughs at you: you can
tell her Master Slender has married her daughter.*

MISTRESS PAGE
[Aside] Doctors doubt that: if Anne Page be my
daughter, she is, by this, Doctor Caius' wife.

*Doctors doubt that: if Anne Page is my
daughter, she is, by this time, Doctor Caius' wife.*

Enter SLENDER

SLENDER
Whoa ho! ho, father Page!

Hello there! Hey, father Page!

PAGE
Son, how now! how now, son! have you
dispatched?

*Son, hello there! Hello, my son! Have you done the
business?*

SLENDER
Dispatched! I'll make the best in Gloucestershire
know on't; would I were hanged, la, else.

*I've been done! I'll let the best people in
Gloucestershire
know about it; otherwise let me be hanged.*

PAGE
Of what, son?

About what, son?

SLENDER
I came yonder at Eton to marry Mistress Anne Page,
and she's a great lubberly boy. If it had not been
i' the church, I would have swinged him, or he
should have swinged me. If I did not think it had
been Anne Page, would I might never stir!--and 'tis
a postmaster's boy.

*I went over to Eton to marry Mistress Anne Page,
and she turned out to be a great hulking lad. If we
hadn't been in the church, I would have thrashed
him, or he would have thrashed me. I swear I
thought it was Anne Page–
and it was the postman's boy!*

PAGE
Upon my life, then, you took the wrong.

Well I swear, you must've taken a wrong turn.

SLENDER
What need you tell me that? I think so, when I took
a boy for a girl. If I had been married to him, for
all he was in woman's apparel, I would not have had
him.

*I don't need you to tell me that. I knew it when I
mistook a boy for a girl. If I had married him, even
though he was dressed as a woman, I would not
have had him.*

PAGE
Why, this is your own folly. Did not I tell you how
you should know my daughter by her garments?

*Why, this is your own stupidity. Didn't I tell you
how to identify my daughter by her clothes?*

SLENDER
I went to her in white, and cried 'mum,' and she
cried 'budget,' as Anne and I had appointed; and yet

*I went to the one in white, and said 'mum,' and she
replied 'budget,' as Anne and I had arranged; and*

it was not Anne, but a postmaster's boy.

MISTRESS PAGE
Good George, be not angry: I knew of your
purpose;
turned my daughter into green; and, indeed, she is
now with the doctor at the deanery, and there
married.

Enter DOCTOR CAIUS

DOCTOR CAIUS
Vere is Mistress Page? By gar, I am cozened: I ha'
married un garcon, a boy; un paysan, by gar, a boy;
it is not Anne Page: by gar, I am cozened.

MISTRESS PAGE
Why, did you take her in green?

DOCTOR CAIUS
Ay, by gar, and 'tis a boy: by gar, I'll raise all
Windsor.

Exit

FORD
This is strange. Who hath got the right Anne?

PAGE
My heart misgives me: here comes Master Fenton.

Enter FENTON and ANNE PAGE

How now, Master Fenton!

ANNE PAGE
Pardon, good father! good my mother, pardon!

PAGE
Now, mistress, how chance you went not with
Master Slender?

MISTRESS PAGE
Why went you not with master doctor, maid?

FENTON
You do amaze her: hear the truth of it.
You would have married her most shamefully,
Where there was no proportion held in love.
The truth is, she and I, long since contracted,

yet it was not Anne, but the postman's boy.

*Good George, don't be angry: I knew what you
were up to;
I changed my daughter's clothes to green; and, in
fact, she is now with the doctor at the chapel, where
she has married him.*

*Where is Mistress Page? By God, I have been
cheated: I have married un garcon, a boy; a
peasant, by God, a boy;
it is not Anne Page: by God, I have been cheated.*

Why, did you take the one in green?

*Yes, by God, and it's a boy: by God, I'll get all
Windsor out of bed.*

This is strange. Who has got the real Anne?

*I'm starting to get worried: here comes Master
Fenton.*

Hello there, Master Fenton!

*Forgive me, good father! My good mother, forgive
me!*

*Now, mistress, why did you not go with Master
Slender?*

Why did you not go with master doctor, maid?

*You are bewildering her: here's the story.
You would have married her in a very shameful
way, where there was no love. The truth is that she
and I, who have been engaged for ages,*

Are now so sure that nothing can dissolve us.
The offence is holy that she hath committed;
And this deceit loses the name of craft,
Of disobedience, or unduteous title,
Since therein she doth evitate and shun
A thousand irreligious cursed hours,
Which forced marriage would have brought upon
her.

FORD
Stand not amazed; here is no remedy:
In love the heavens themselves do guide the state;
Money buys lands, and wives are sold by fate.

FALSTAFF
I am glad, though you have ta'en a special stand to
strike at me, that your arrow hath glanced.

PAGE
Well, what remedy? Fenton, heaven give thee joy!
What cannot be eschew'd must be embraced.

FALSTAFF
When night-dogs run, all sorts of deer are chased.

MISTRESS PAGE
Well, I will muse no further. Master Fenton,
Heaven give you many, many merry days!
Good husband, let us every one go home,
And laugh this sport o'er by a country fire;
Sir John and all.

FORD
Let it be so. Sir John,
To Master Brook you yet shall hold your word
For he tonight shall lie with Mistress Ford.

Exeunt

are now joined so tight that nothing can tear us apart.
She has committed a holy sin;
and this trickery cannot be called cunning,
or disobedience, or lack of duty,
since by doing it she has avoided and rejected
a thousand hours of unholy behaviour
which a forced marriage would have brought her.

Don't be bewildered; there's nothing to be done:
the heavens themselves guide the path of love;
money buys land, wives are given by destiny.

I'm glad, although you have made a special effort
to shoot at me, that you didn't hit the target full on.

Well, what can be done? Fenton, may heaven bring
you happiness!
What can't be cured must be endured.

When you hunt in the night, you don't always get the
game you expected.

Well, I have no more complaints. Master Fenton,
may heaven give you many many happy days!
Good husband, let's all go home,
and have a laugh about these games by a country
fire; Sir John and all.

Let's do that. Sir John,
you will still keep your promise to Master Brook,
because tonight he shall sleep with Mistress Ford.

Made in the USA
Middletown, DE
17 December 2016